The Battle For Life

By: Dr. Earl W. Lacy

The Battle For Life

Copyright © 2011

By: Dr. Earl W. Lacy

ISBN-13   978-0 -9970856-4-8
ISBN-10   09970856-4-9

Printed in the United States of America
By: Ecclesia Publishing House
ecclesiapublishinghouse.com

Table of Contents

Preface

It is for freedom that Christ has set us free. This is the heart and purpose of His sacrifice at Calvary. True freedom includes the release from the control and expectations of family, friends and even church folks; freedom from sicknesses, diseases, poverty and the molestation of unclean spirits.

I for one do not want to go to Hell, but neither do I want to be trampled on, abused by demons while I am alive either! So, there are promises and provisions in the Word of God that gives us, the Believer in Christ Jesus authority over unclean spirits, to cast them out, and to heal all manner of sicknesses, diseases and infirmities; plus all the generational curses such as poverty, that He took away and nailed to the cross.

The Apostle Paul wrote that the good things that he wanted to do, instead he did the opposite; he said that evil was always present to prevent him from doing the right thing--- but he didn't leave it at that. Paul wrote that the Law of the Spirit of Life in Christ Jesus made him free of the Law of Sin and Death that works through the flesh. **The Battle For Life** is to take hold and live in the Law of the Spirit of Life. Herein, is the key to the freedom we all seek after.

It is easy for me to write about a subject that is close to my heart. For in my life I have played the part of a fool, and have erred exceedingly; I have done my share of sinning. Many times in this book you will read that I use the words "we" "us" and "our" to make the paragraphs more personal, to bring it home to the reader. For I was once an un-Saved sinner, but now a Christian Saved by Grace through Faith;

now a member of the Five-Fold Ministry, and have been a follower of other church leaders throughout my Christian Journey---so many of the statements made in this book also apply to me.

Today we are made aware of prominent Christian Ministers who have fallen into public disgrace because some particular sin was revealed in their lives. When this happens the secular world the secular world reaffirms their belief that we are a bunch of hypocrites, and the churches kick that minister to the curb! Many "baby" Christians who followed him or her stumbles and falls to the side because their confidence was more in the minister than in Christ, the Word of God.

This book explains the reason why so many ministers and church goers find it difficult if not impossible to live the Christian lifestyle that is pleasing to God; not the lifestyles pleasing to themselves or their denominations.

I pray that the reader will take to heart what I have written. The majority of the information is from the Holy Bible, the Word of God; other information is from my life experiences, successes and failures, personal struggles with sin, counseling others---including criminals.

Because I'm a simple down-to-earth-man is why I believe God used me to write this simple down-to-earth book. I am not now, and never have been a perfect man, but I sought and received the Grace and Mercy of God through Inner Healing and Deliverance for myself. Still other information comes from my 59+ years of living in this sin-cursed world, and working in the Ministry of Inner Healing and Deliverance.

The purpose that I have written this book is not to expose the sin in the local churches, but to help all Christians to understand the true meaning and divine spiritual destiny that is appointed, approved and made available to us in freedom "If the Son therefore shall make you free, you shall be free indeed"---John 8.36.

Dr. Earl W. Lacy   January 27, 2016

THE BATTLE FOR LIFE
CHAPTER ONE

THE UNDERGROUND RAILROAD

"Now faith is being sure of what we hope for and certain of what we do not see"--- Heb. 11.1 (NIV)

From the time the first shipload of defiant Negros landed in the market places and auction blocks of the old South, and from the cradle to the grave, long days of forced labor, humiliation and suffering was the testimony of thousands of Africans who were victimized, uprooted from families and exploited because of the color of their skin and their primitive tribal cultures.

Thus of necessity and moral responsibility to these lost souls in bondage, the Underground Railroad became a network of both black and white citizens who helped fugitive slaves to escape from the South to the free North. Through a system of safe houses, it was estimated that between the years 1810-1850 over 100,000 slaves were set free.

The system or society of "patriots" was secretly formed towards the end of the 18th century, when in 1786 George Washington, a slave owner himself, complained about how one of his runaway slaves was assisted to escape by what he suspected was a "society of Quakers."

Around 1831 when the steam engine and the business/corporation called the railroad came to be the mode of mass transit, then the name "Underground Railroad" was given to this secret society. Using the railroad terminology, the homes and businesses where the fugitives rested were called "stations," "depots" and were run by "stationmasters." Those who contributed food and clean clothing to the fugitives were "stockholders," and the "conductor" moved the fugitives from one station to the next. Often a conductor would sneak onto a plantation. Posing as a slave, he would convince the actual slaves to follow him or her to freedom; they would stirrup and activate faith.

Yet, on many occasions, the conductor found himself or herself in peril, because hundreds, perhaps even thousands of slaves refused freedom; they were victims of being "institutionalized" or "brainwashed" into believing in their utter worthlessness, helplessness, inferiority, blackness, low-birth self-esteem; they sincerely believed that they were the master's property without a say in their own destiny; these were those who betrayed the plans of the conductors and those who would escape because they cherished freedom.

Ironically, even during the height of the Civil War, many Negros served in the Confederate Army, because they were promised freedom when the South won the war; but, the demonic deception, the thinking distortion upon them---that they would be free if they escaped to the North or fought in the Union Army to defeat the tyrants of the South! It is mind-boggling how the slaves believed that their slave masters were honest and had their best interest at heart!

Other times, the master sent armed men with bloodhounds to track them down through the swamps, woods and farm-lands and bring the runaways back; for a fee, there were also bounty hunters who specialized in tracking down and returning runaway slaves to the Southern plantation owners.

The Underground Railroad had many leaders and participants; a few were John Fairfield in Ohio, Levi Coffin, a Quaker who assisted more than 3,000 slaves, and Harriet

Tubman, who made 19 trips into the South and rescued over 300 slaves. Harriet Tubman was a no-nonsense woman who threatened to kill a slave who started out with her and then wanted to change their mind about escaping.

The desire to be free is already instilled in the hearts of all mankind; a Negro slave was no different; but the motivation, the will to lay it all on the line to obtain the goal of freedom was a different matter. Some would rather be a live slave than a dead runaway. The fear of failure was greater than their hope of success. But for others, their faith was the subject of things they hoped for, the evidence of the freedom not seen, but believed; their faith "believing" was real fact what was not yet manifested to their outward senses; hope of being free at last was where their faith was---it was FREEDOM---or die trying!

Even in the cotton and tobacco fields of the South, the Negros sang spiritual songs—-gospel songs of freedom; not only freedom in the hereafter, but a NOW freedom.....while still living in the mortal body. These Spirit-led songs prepared their hearts to deal with their everyday world-slave life, the Battle of Life, which would ultimately lead to the **Battle For Life**, which they had not yet experienced prior to Salvation. In this rest the freedom and authority in the Natural and Spirit Realm---not only a battle to get saved but one to stay that way!

GOD'S SPECIAL FORCES

"It is for freedom that Christ has set us free. Stand firm, then, and do not let your-self be burdened again by a yoke of slavery"---Gal. 5.1 (NIV).

It is interesting to note that a bird caged for a long period of time, suddenly sees the door opened wide will just look at it and not fly away: So is the above mentioned account of many slaves who refused to be set free by the conductors of the Underground Railroad; in fact some had exposed the escape plans, because they were more loyal to their master and his system of control and rules then they were with the greater idea of being free to make their own life decisions.

And so it is with the general population of the world who loves the self-life of natural things, clothes, food, entertainment, alcohol, drugs, sex and other self gratifications; this is the slave-world-system mentality that originated with the prince of this world, Satan---who is the master of this entire world plantation!

Today the Underground Railroad is not to free African slaves, the men, women, boys and girls from working in the cotton fields (though child labor and human trafficking is still a negative reality), but to free humanity from the owner of the entire world-plantation, who uses mankind like chess pieces in a game to capture all of us and take us with him to Hell.

The conductors are God's Special Forces Team; they are equipped with the Sword of the Spirit as the weapon, the Shield of Faith, the Helmet of Salvation, and feet ready to rush into battle with the Gospel of Peace (2 Cor. 10.4) . These weapons are not forged by a blacksmith or by a ninja warrior, but their designer and Craftsman is God. And their power to slice through the darkness also originates with God, who created all things by and through Jesus Christ.

The prince of this world is not concerned with the color of our skin; he is an equal opportunity destroyer of lives. In the same way many of the slaves opposed freedom and those who thirsted for it, desired it, and had great passion for it--- Satan uses family, friends, associates and "religious" folks who claim that they are "Christian" to keep those who desire to draw nearer to the fullness of freedom, into an intimate, personal relationship with Christ from achieving that goal.

The stations and depots are the places of refuge that we call the local churches. There, the stationmaster, the pastor, is responsible for our spiritual growth; to teach the doctrines to raise us up as spiritual sons and daughters (and not to just get all our money through cleverly devised sermons and guilt trips—discussed in a later chapter). The pastor is to nurture and raise us up to continue the good fight of faith against the entrenched army of Satan.

As the conductors went into the plantation at great risk to their own safety, so does God's Special Forces Team go into the unsaved world and lead those who are willing to give up their chains and heavy burdens for the promise of Eternal Life, to take back the people who belong to God from Satan who stole the entire world and everyone and thing in it from Adam, the created Man who received the world and authority to rule it from God (Gen. 1.26).

In the same way the Southern plantation owners issued a Warrant and a Wanted Poster, then employed armed Bounty Hunters with dogs to bring back the runaway slaves, and to return dead or alive those who helped them escape---Satan sends forth demons to bring back those who escaped from his world-system to live a life with Jesus Christ; and to bring back, dead or alive, the ministers of Christ, the Special Forces Team, who helped them to escape, and those who are harboring the fugitives in the local churches. He uses former temptations, addictions, mind-sets, mental strongholds, soul ties, blood ties, friends and business associates; he also uses the mass media to reach the minds of the runaways; he also aggravates preexisting medical and mental conditions in hopes of quenching the love, joy and peace of those In Jesus Christ, whereby decreasing the quality of life for all the escaped Christians.

It is evident that all Christians need extensive Inner Healing and Deliverance to deal with the past abuse, generational curses, blood curses and brainwashing that occurred even while we were innocent in our mother's womb. From the time we breathed our first breath, a demon familiar spirit was assigned to see to it that we remained a slave to this world; and we are also living under the watchful eyes of the world spirits----at times, they are quiet and subtle but can become violent and explosive in disposition and enforcement---especially over major cities, third-world countries and terrorists havens. They rule the geographical territories where we live (Eph. 610-12).

When a man escapes from the County Jail or prison, immediately alarms sound and the authorities responsible for that man's incarceration spring into action to look for him; the goal is to return him to serve his sentence, and to punish him even further for his refusal to stay incarcerated. If the person is particularly dangerous, a murderer or the like, the police tells its officers to "proceed with caution" and "may be armed and dangerous" and "use deadly force if necessary to apprehend."

The first place the police will go is to the man's last known address. If his relatives, spouse or girlfriend is there, they are questioned extensively about the fugitive. Satisfied that the escapee isn't there, the next place they look is his known hangouts and the people he associated with before he was jailed. Following up on those leads and armed with the famous All Points Bulletin (APB) they enlist the FBI, State Police and other law enforcement agencies; they may also use the media to help them bring the fugitive to justice.

And so it is with Satan and his horde: He will attempt to use our spouse relatives, friends, church members, courts, associates or media; he will enlist people from our past and lure us back to our old sinful way of thinking---hangouts, clubs and toxic people to get us back into his custody, where he can keep us from being all that we are called to be In Christ.

But once real spiritual freedom is experienced and obtained, returning to slavery---whether physical or spiritual, is no longer an option: The Apostle Paul said "For to me to live is Christ, to die is gain" (Phil. 1.21).

THE BATTLE OF LIFE

"Therefore, I say unto you, Take no thought for your life, what ye shall eat, or what ye shall drink; nor yet for your body, what ye shall put on. **Is not the life more** than meat, and the body than raiment?"---Mat. 6.25(KJV).

The Plantation slaves not only had to work long hours in the hot sun, but the living arrangements and quality of life in general by any standard were appalling. But though they were physically poor, many were spiritually rich, because their hope was in Jesus and not in the plantation, or in the escape to the North.

Yes, it is for certain that they dreamed of walking down the street as a free person, or having an actual paying job with pocket money to sit and order hot food in a restaurant; to order a steak with mashed potatoes, gravy, corn on the cob and other side dishes; the women dreamed of shopping for clothing in the fancy boutiques and dressing their children with new not tattered and repaired clothing; they dreamed of sending their children to school to learn how to read and write; and finally they dreamed of being able to hold their heads high and be respected as a human being, equal to those with white completion.

The battle of (natural) life begins with the struggle to take our first breath. When our eyes open for the first time and we are ushered into a world of lights and loud sounds made by those who had already been here a long time. We gulp in the air then down the first bottle of milk formula that was given to us, or went to work on our mother's nipple as she offered it to feed us. Our instincts were to get all we can as fast as we can because our behavior was mostly instinct, and we didn't know that there was more where that came from. We fought or first battle of life: Self Preservation; but the most important battle, the Battle for Life remained an invisible struggle to be realized later.

It is easy to conform to the world. From the time of birth, most of us are brought home by parents who are conformed to thinking according to the status quo, the world system of values; then comes the relatives, friends, school books and television that "instruct" us in how to be like everyone else---how to fit in and find your niche in society. If we do not conform enough, we are called weird, strange, or voted "less likely to succeed"---perhaps called a loser!

It is not so easy to be a spiritual person in this world; even the before mentioned Principalities, Powers and Rulers of the Darkness, the Spiritual Wickedness in the Heavenies (Eph. 6.10-12) would look down in anger and dispatch a demon or two, or a love one of ours to put us back in our place, and thus bring conformity to our life, the old fashioned way---by manipulation, intimidation and domination, that is, witchcraft.

Is not the Life more than physical needs? Is what Jesus asked His audience? Is it more than the best food, home, car, career, spouse, billions of dollars, popularity or position? Thousands of people who were born poor but are now rich would conclude: Rich is better! Jesus didn't say that we cannot have riches, but admonishes us to understand that Life is more than physical wealth. And so the lesson is---don't worry yourself to death---literally stroke-out about these things; because in the same way He feeds and takes care of the birds, He will do even more for a human being, especially one who seeks first the Kingdom and its righteousness, and believes by Faith that His promises are true.

Many of us are too caught up in looking good, the outer appearance, when God is looking on the heart. There is nothing wrong with taking care of our physical body or even the mental soul-life inside the body, but we are discussing the excessive conformity to the world. We want to look fabulous all the time and shop to we drop.

We spend thousands of dollars a year on clothes, cosmetics, surgurical procedures including breast implants, Indian Hair pieces, high heel shoes; and the men spend generously on suits and luxury vehicles; we decorate our flesh like a Christmas tree, and are barely if ever concerned about the pursuit of Holiness, the other Life, called Eternal Life.

It is because many churchgoers believe that we already have Eternal Life---so why pursue or fight for something that we already have? Therefore, armed with that realization, we strut into church like we are doing God a favor in going. When the time comes we throw a few dollars in the offering plate, as though giving God a tip for being a good waiter, and leave out with renewed energy to continue the battle of life---to get all that we can before we die---as though it were a game of competition.

Salvation is a work in progress; Sanctification is the process in which the Holy Spirit transforms our mind from being conformed to the world and its standards. The mind, being conformed to the world and driven by the flesh to stay that way, is also influenced by the demonic powers.

The Battle for (Eternal) Life also began at birth; for it is God's plan that we obtain Salvation through Jesus Christ. And it is Satan's plan that we die without obtaining Salvation. If he can't stop us, he will fight to the end to get us to let go of God's protective hands, and so we have to fight to stay Saved and live a life that is pleasing to God (The "once Saved, always Saved" is doctoral theory and religious error; it was introduced by preachers who wanted to continue to live in their "secret" sins. This is discussed in a later chapter).

In the Physical World exist different kinds of natural life: Scientists study animal and plant life, microscopic life forms including bacteria, fungi and viruses. The Medical Profession deal with many microscopic life forms that invade the human body. Their goal is to improve the quality of human health by creating new drugs and vaccines to fight infections, and thus improve the natural life so that human beings will live a better and longer life span. This is a noble cause.

Since the first human being caught a cold, the need for medicine began. And since then, leprosy, AIDS, cancers, deformities and other horrible diseases arose in epidemic proportions. Scientists rush to find cures or at least slow down the infection rate of the disease, even temporarily eliminate the pain, and therefore comfort the inflicted until the disease finally terminates the natural body.

When a disease like Cancer consumes the physical body to the extent that it cannot function or survive, it is said that the person "lost their fight with cancer." But the natural life is not all there is to being a human being; and the Medical Doctors are not the only ones whose goal is to heal the sick: God is able and willing to heal the sick. He is also the one who offers the second Life: Eternal Life.

The battle of life, (which is part of the War: Good versus Evil) like the battlefield of the mind, takes its toll on the physical body as well as the Mental or Soul Body. The Soul is the Mind, Will, Emotions and Imagination (creative processes). Trials, tribulations, situations, circumstances, bills, sickness and deaths make life at times intolerable and quite painful---not to mention living with another 6.7 billion people who are going through the same things! But there is hope in fighting the good fight of Faith and laying hold of Salvation.

LIFE IS MERELY A VAPOR

8 "With the Lord, a day is like a thousand years, and a thousand years is like a day. 13 Now listen, you say, "Today or tomorrow we will go to this or that city, spend a year there, carry on business and make money." 14 Why, you do not even know what will happen tomorrow. What is your life? **You are merely a vapor** that appears for a while and then vanishes" 2 Pet. 3.8; James 4.13, 14 (NIV).

This is a chilling realization if considered in its biblical context. To God, a thousand years is like a day. The oldest man recorded in the Old Testament, Methuselah lived 969 years (Gen. 5.27) before he died. So Methuselah fell 31 years short of living one day of the Lord, a thousand years. So the natural life is considerably temporary compared to the concept of eternity.

The average lifespan in the developed countries is around 70 years old. So, what are we doing with this life? What are our plans, purposes and pursuits? And what is the purpose of such a temporary existence on this third planet from the sun? And, lastly, where do we go when this life is over; when the physical body is too old to continue, sickness or tragedy robs us of what life and years we could have had? Can we go to the store and buy another physical body? The truth is we didn't but the one we have! It is a gift from God.

The Apostle James addresses many of these concerns. We make a lot of bold plans in consideration that we will be alive to implement them! It is not in itself wrong to make plans, but like many of us, we do not consider how impermanent our stay here is. We are living in the physical world as spiritual beings not of this world; we are not entirely physical beings living in the physical world and seeking to have a spiritual awakening or relationship with our Creator. The fact that many people do not believe this statement doesn't negate its reality; the fact that atheists do not believe in God or even that they are spirit beings doesn't change the spiritual-material or even the matter-energy composition of the universe.

As stated earlier, our concerns over creature-comfort have driven many to be more occupied with looking and smelling good that our concern for the spirit-man is all but forgotten. Self-centeredness, pride, vanity and greed have plagued even the churches of God. There are a hundred times more sermons about money generated by preachers (not the Holy Spirit) than the Fruit of the Spirit (character) or Spiritual Gifts (Healing, Prophecy, Miracles etc.). And this is because these ministries consider making money for themselves the top priority (more in a later chapter). Apostle James was concerned about such plans.

Apostle James stated that life is a vapor. There is an old saying "Here today, gone tomorrow". That statement is only partially true. Here today, gone today, or here one minute, gone the next is more accurate. We all know people who were happy and talking one day, and then we hear that they died a few hours ago from a heart attack or automobile accident. Life is so fragile, so unpredictable. It behooves up to use our "vapor" wisely, to make our life here count for more than looking good, fancy cars, drugs, alcohol, random sex, business, careers or other excessive compulsive behaviors such as gambling or criminal activities. Why not live a life that is pleasing to God and of lasting benefit to our children and others? Why not leave a legacy of compass-sionate service to God and those around us? Then when it is time to leave this world it is a Home Going and not a funeral; one is Heaven bound and the other straight to Hell.

Vapor, like fog, comes in the night when the conditions are right, stays on the ground until the sun comes up and it melts away. The same is the case with smoke; it rises and dissipates when the wind scatters it. Apostle James used the vapor example well. He was not saying that the natural life is unimportant, meaningless, or shouldn't be taken seriously, but only that it was temporary.

EVENING COMES TO US ALL

"That day when evening came, He said to his disciples, "Let us go over to the other side"---Mark 4.35 (NIV).

Apostle Mark wrote of a particular evening when Jesus ushered the disciples into a boat and they set out to cross the sea. A great storm arose while they were at sea. The waves beat against the ship and it was taking on water. These were trained fishermen; they had been on the sea and most likely through many storms. Sudden storms often came up. They really believed that this storm would be the death of them all. While this was taking place, Jesus was peacefully asleep.

The boat represents our journey from birth to physical death. All the members of this particular boat are in the Presence of Jesus. He is in the boat and not excited about this storm or any storm that suddenly appears and threaten our security In Him. He is not reluctant to demonstrate His exceedingly great power to declare and decree "Peace, be still!"

Our life in this world is like a single day; not a day of the Lord, but a 24 hr. day:

12:01 a.m. We are born, helpless and frightened. We need someone to care for us, love us, feed us and protect us. We also need parents to teach us how to live in this new world of sights, sounds and smells. We are innocent, in that we have done nothing to bring ourselves into this world. God assigns guardian angels to watch over us; but Satan also assigns evil spirits to oppose those angels, with assignments to activate generational curses, including sicknesses, and by any means necessary, keep us from accepting Jesus Christ.

9:00 a.m. We are a child, bold and adventurous, going to school, developing friendships and a sense of where we fit in; we are learning how to conform to this world. Many of our Christian parents or relatives took us to church. There in Sunday School we learned what God says is good or evil thoughts and behaviors; but at this age, temptations are few, though we are told to look both ways before crossing the street, made aware that there are sexual predators, and we shouldn't take rides from strangers (or certain relatives either!).

Nevertheless, the sights, sounds and glamour of what the world can offer is alluring---even the video games are exceptionally addictive, violent and blood-thirsty; we text our friends and talk on the phone because consumes most of our free time. There is also little time to do those things that the Bible recommends: Praying and reading Scriptures. We are reminded that spiritual things are more important than material things, but it seems that there is a battle raging in our mind to accept the material over the spiritual. Yet, to others our age, there doesn't seem to be any conflict: To them, the material is better.

12:01 p.m. We are teenagers. We notice our individuality and express it with our vocal preferences and decisions; we are individuals and sometimes rebellious to parents and teachers alike. We get caught up in our feelings and emotions; the flesh raises up in pursuit of love, company-ionship, money, material things, pleasure, entertainment, popularity, and habits like sex, smoking cigarettes, drinking alcohol and smoking marijuana.

Some of us do not know what hour it is, nor how much Jesus loves us and wants to be a part of our life. He is waiting for us to believe, trust, and rely on Him as our personal Lord and Savior; He stands at the door and knocks! But those evil spirits are now a great influence in our life; it is as though they are inside our head---and having a board meeting every morning to decide how they would waste more of our life, and keep us preoccupied until it is time to leave this world---preferably without Christ in our life.

3:00 p.m. We are an adult. Perhaps we suffer from years of situations and circumstance in and out of our control: Mental, physical and sexual abuse, betrayal, abandonment, rejection, divorce, child death, parent death, alcoholism, drug addiction, suicide attempts, imprisonments, sicknesses, unemployment and other calamities. At times life has been unbearable; it was not what we thought it was going to be! But it's almost over; at least---the physical part of it.

Perhaps, we have considered Jesus Christ but have not accepted Him; or we did accept Him as a child but then went about our life without Him; or, as many claim, we were hesitate to attend church because of the lifestyles of some Christians that we know, or the public disgrace of several prominent television ministers (who, by the way, didn't die on the cross for anyone!) and we felt that if Jesus Christ couldn't help them live honorable lives, how could He help us?

Be that as it may---one thing that we have noticed is that we are getting old and tired. We have outlived most of our friends; we are older but not wiser---still unsaved or in a backslidden condition. But as the years go by we have become restless, even fearful of what awaits us on the other side, the end of the journey.

6:00 p.m. We are a Senior Citizen. We are eligible for a lot of discounts: Social Security, pension, 401K, food, medical insurance, auto insurance and other benefits. However, the long wait for these benefits was not worth it! Perhaps we have been sick a few times, or are terminally ill, or in a convalescent home. Yet by the grace of God we are still in this world. We look back over our life and maybe our good days outweigh our bad days.

We often think about our genealogical accomplishments, our children, grandchildren and great grandchildren, and we are proud of these.. But we are in the boat of life, and the boat will not stop until it reaches its destination. We know deep in our heart that our sins must be forgiven before we reach the other side; we must be washed from a lifetime of corruption and sin, because if our physical body dies and we end up on that distant shore without Jesus Christ in the boat---it would have been better not to be born at all!

9:00 p.m. Evening has come; the boat has docked on the other side. Life in this world is over; it's time to face God to answer one profound question. It will not be how much money did you make? How many children? Were you popular? How are you Mr. President? Or what church title did you have? No, it will be: Did you accept Jesus Christ as your Savior and Lord?

Jesus taught about the importance of family and relationships. The right relationship with God this side of the grave makes all the difference; it determines the quality of life in this world and the next. There is a Friend who sticks to us closer than a brother: His Name is Jesus Christ. No other Friend can carry us through life's storms and howling winds; carry us across the raging situations and circumstances into Eternal Life, a prepared place.

Through Jesus and Him only we have forgiveness of sins, help in this world and access to Heaven. We should diligently guard against the desires of the flesh, the human nature without the Holy Spirit within, and the expectation of demon spirits who would persuade us that the world has more to offer, more frills and thrills, than Christ. Jesus said: "For what shall it profit a man, if he shall gain the whole world and lose his own soul? Or what shall a man give in exchange for his soul?" (Mk. 8.36,37).

Notes

CHAPTER TWO
IN HIM IS LIFE

1. "In the beginning {before all time} was the Word (Christ), and the Word was with God, and the Word was God Himself. 3. All things were made and came into existence through Him.....4. In Him was Life, and the Life was the Light of men. 5. And the Light shines on in the darkness, for the darkness has never overpowered it {put it out or absorbed it or appropriated it, and is unreceptive to it}" --- Jn. 1.1,3,4,5 (Amp. Bible).

In the previous chapter the subject of natural, physical or mortal life was expounded upon. The quality and quantity of human life and personal freedoms was also discussed in detail---including the joys, pleasures, achievements, trage-dies and human misery that often accompanies living as a terrestrial being.

Now that the battle of life has been clearly defined, now it is time to discuss the battle to obtain and hold on to a different kind of Life: Eternal Life.

Apostle John in explaining who Jesus Christ is, began with, "In the beginning," which is the correct place to start when talking about this kind of Life. He wrote that before all time was the Word, who is also the Person called Christ. This Christ was with God as a member of a Trinity (Father, Son, Holy Spirit). Yet, all things were made and came into existence through Christ. It was In Him that this (Eternal) Life exists, and the Life could lift and restore fallen persons---us, to the heights of heavenly dignity and fellowship with the Father as though we had always been with Him and never were separated because of sin.

The Light is the radiance, the outflow of the Life of God. The Life of Christ is the same Life that keeps God and the other members of the Trinity alive; this Life is what makes them eternal: Omnipotent, Omniscient and Omnipresent--- God.

The Life of Christ is so powerful, the darkness, Satan and his demonic government has never overpowered the Life, or quenched the Life---nor is he capable of benefiting from the Life, use the Life or redirect the Life; in fact, since his fall from Heaven, Satan cannot even understand how the Spirit of Life even works (because the Spirit of Life is also the Person called the Holy Spirit). And thus Satan wars against God and the intelligent Spirit-Life that flows from the Throne of God and Christ, as Christ supplies the needs of those who call upon His Name.

Apostle John further testified as a witness concerning the Light, that all men through him might believe: That the Light, Life, Word, Christ was incarnating into the world of human beings as a human being, and whosoever believes in Him, trust in and relied on His Word, would have the authority, right and rank on earth and Heaven, to be called sons (and daughters) of God.

Believers would receive His Life-Spirit, inward likeness and character that is in the image of God. They would receive Him in their once dead or unresponsive human spirit; by a quickening, being made alive and conscious by the Life-giving Presence of the Holy Spirit of Christ. And once being conscious and awakened, the human spirit would once again be aware of its Creator, love Him, praise and worship Him, communicate with Him, and assist Him in His overall plan for the redemption of mankind.

The Word became flesh, a human being known as Jesus of Nazareth. He pitched his tent of flesh, tabernacle and made His abode among us. The entrance of the Word brought

Light (ps. 119.130). The Word brought under-standing and intuition, the ability of the human spirit to "know" without studying the will of God, His plans, purposes and pursuits.

Jesus said to His audience in John 8.12 "I AM the Light of the world; he that follows Me shall not walk in darkness, but shall have the Light of Life. Here the Savior, as John did, used the terms Light and Life to emphasize that the radiance of the Light is in proportion or direct relationship to the Life that is within; that because the Spirit of Christ dwells within us, there should be corresponding fruit or evidence of His Presence. Jesus also says it this way: "Ye {we} are the Light of the world. A city that is on a hill cannot be hid. Neither do men light a candle, and put it under a bushel, but on a candlestick...Let your Light so shine before men, that they may see your good works, and glorify your Father which is in heaven."

When we receive the Holy Spirit in our human spirit, a transformation and awakening takes place; our spirit is awakened from its slumber and filled with the radiance, Light and Life of Christ. Once empowered, we walk the earth as new creatures (unregenerate people are human spirit, soul, and physical body or three-part beings. Christians are Holy Spirit, human spirit, soul, and physical body or four-part beings---a new creation.). So, Jesus was saying, with all this Light and Life within, don't hide the Life but do good works so that the Father will receive glory and others will want what we have.

"Therefore if any man be in Christ, he is a new creature: old things are passed away; behold all things are become new" (2 Cor. 5.17). This is a familiar scripture to many and quoted widely. We are new creatures because we have God's Spirit dwelling in us and we belong to His family. We are no longer the plantation slaves of the world, but have been given the ministry of reconciliation. We are ambassadors for Christ, and we are to persuade people to come out of the darkness and demonic activity into the Light and Life of Christ. The old Egyptian slave mentality, even the grave clothes of the past, must be shed at the Jordan River or left in the tomb like Lazarus' stinky grave clothes.

The Battle of Life continues. The enemy of our soul, though he tried to kill us many times, failed in those attempts and we made it by the grace of God, prayers of other Christians and the protection of the guardian angels; our angels of God who fight many unseen battles but sometimes are overwhelmed with the tremendous hordes of evil spirits executing maneuvers and operations between Hell and on earth; many people perish at their evil hands before they get a chance to accepted Christ, the Life; still others, motivated by demonized flesh, kill themselves with drugs, alcohol and hazardous lifestyles and never find Christ.

Now that we are children of God, the enemy has stepped up his attacks. As stated earlier, we are fugitives from the world system. We have dared to defy the ruling spirits over the geographical area in which we live, not to mention the thousands of demons and human being they use to keep the sin going in and around us. We have declared war against the enemy of our soul!

Jesus said in John 10.10, "The thief comes not, but to steal, and to kill, and to destroy: I Am come that they might have Life, and that they might have it more abundantly." The thief, meaning Satan, was a murderer from the beginning. When he comes to steal, he is not really after our material possessions, though he may play mind games by interfering with our finances---but his real goal is to enslave our soul and to keep us away from God; his tactic is to return us to the former state before we received the Life of Christ. He doesn't want us to have the abundant Life, whereby we worship God. No, he is not after our 72 inch color television or our new car---he wants our worship and conformity to the world.

"And be not conformed to this world, but be ye transformed by the renewing of the mind, that you may prove what is that good, and acceptable and perfect will of God" Rom. 12.2. This is just one of many Scriptures that instruct us that there is something evil and severely wrong with the world system of thought, belief and behaviors. The Word also refers to "former conversations, "the stuff we used to talk about and places we used to go because it was important to us.

The flesh, or the mind of the flesh is called the "old man" who is corrupt and deceitful and full of unredeemable qualities. The flesh cannot be rehabilitated, improved, "churched", shamed into behaving or changed by mental health experts---except drugged until harmless and also senseless. It has to experience death at the cross, so the "inner man" of the heart can make himself known.

In this crooked and perverse world, we are to shine as Light and Life to the world. But the demonic powers dissuade us daily, and we must continuously take a stand for Christ and the Life He has instilled in us.

OUR SECRET SINS

"That is, they which are the children of the flesh, these are not the children of God: But the children of the Promise are counted for the Seed (Christ)--- Rom.9.8.

A few ways we quench the Light and Life of Christ in us:

Quench the Holy Spirit by ignoring His promptings: We often to need to see miracles, signs and wonders before we budge to do something that God wants done, or to purchase a book that will help us to understand the will of God; we require multiple witnesses and prophets to confirm what we already know is the will of God (because we really don't want to do it); but somehow we don't feel "lead" to pray and seek Godly counsel before we slide our Visa Card to purchase for ourselves expensive clothes, shoes, cars, furniture, or even to marry a spouse who is often unsaved, neither do we seek God's counsel before having sexual intercourse with a friend; but invoke the imaginary "friends with benefits" clause in the Covenant with Jesus Christ.

Being passive when we should speak up on social issues: We are quiet on moral issues such as abortion, child prostitution, child abuse, spousal abuse, human trafficking, genocide in Sudan and other countries, gang violence, drug dealers, city corruption, prayer taken out of schools/public places, Homosexual and Lesbian marriages, Gays in the pulpit, violence on television, idolizing of movie stars and their non-Christian lifestyles.

Conforming to the world: We do this by going along with the unsaved masses, the popular opinion that is contrary to God's Word. We see starving people in third world countries, and the Spirit is stirred, but we really don't care. We see on video Christians being burned alive and beaten, plus a 17 year old Kurdish girl that was stoned to death for dating a Sunni boy, women imprisoned and beaten in Moslem countries for clothing violations and it doesn't move us, because it's not someone that we personally know.

Denying Christ and being a Christian: We are Christians on Sunday or when it's convenient. Our lifestyle and conversation at home, work or community is no different than the world, and therefore no one is interested in accepting Jesus because we are not an example of someone who they want to become.

Lack of respect for the Person or Ministry of the Holy Spirit: We disrespect and grieve the Holy Spirit by calling Him an "it". We refuse to allow Him to correct our behavior or renew our mind through the Word of God, or even read our Bible, nor do we heed His wooing or warnings.

Not praying: There is little or no striving for a personal, intimate relation-ship with Christ but we settle for a church-relationship, clique or to worship the pastor; we depend on him to pray and seek God, then tell us what He says.

Neither do we seek the fellowship with the Holy Spirit. We also fail by the lack of trying to resist impulses to be lazy and "trust in man" or to avoid premeditated sin. When the Holy Spirit in us checks our behavior, we ignore Him and do what we want to do. We grieve Him when we love the darkness more and rather than the Light, because we love the pleasures of sin for a season. And thus makes the work of the Holy Spirit in us take longer or not take place at all. In the end, we backslide, and might not make it back in time, and if this happens will be lost forever. Included in this is asking ministers to fast for us, during which we eat everything that we can get our hands on!

Ignoring the legitimate needs of others: Having no empathy for the poor, the sick, afflicted or elderly. Having a give-to-me spirit while not giving aid to fellow Christians either. This includes not financially supporting ministers and prayer groups whom we frequently ask for prayer----we burn-up their phone lines with petitions for prophecies, health or financial breakthroughs. But after our prayers are answered, we ignore the minister and ministry who stood in agreement with us, then march into the mega-church that we belong, and throw money and praise at the feet of a bishop and staff members who are seldom if ever available to us, who didn't do anything to assist us, but only want our money, praise and testimony, so others would think that because we belong to their particular ministry is the reason that we got blessed!

Not sharing or witnessing the Gospel to others: This is sometimes attributed to being unskilled in the presentation of the Gospel, but could be avoided by regularly attending Bible Study; it could also be a spirit of fear operating in our life, or a spirit of selfishness, a lack of concern for the lost and their salvation, or even downplaying the seriousness of sin.

Harboring demon spirits: Allowing the frequent manifestations of Unforgiveness, lying, jealousy, racism, hatred, selfishness, addictions, sexual sins, doctoral error and religion; plus the failure to acknowledge that we need help in dealing with these evil spirits, but being self-righteousness refuse to receive Inner Healing/Deliverance when prompted by the Holy Spirit to attend sessions; and being too proud or stubborn to ask and receive Christian Counseling.

Not Tithing or supporting the work of the ministry: Being stingy and robbing God of His money; driving, eating or wearing God's Tithes in order to glamorize ourselves, and thinking more highly of ourselves than we ought to think because of our wealth, occupation or position in the Body of Christ; murmuring and complaining about helping around the church, yet being the first in line for free food!

Lying: Lying to God, the Holy Ghost and to other people. Promising to help people and not doing it; lying to bill collectors, owing people money but refusing to pay them though we are able to pay. This especially includes the extraordinary amount of lying, deceiving, manipulating and crooked business practices and persons who are ministers in the Body of Christ! One would think that the leaders would have grown out of this bad habit, but it is hardly the case! "Lie not one to another, seeing that you have put off the old man with his deeds---Col. 3.9.

We are admonished to walk as children of God. We have His Spirit and His Life. "Know ye not that you are the temple of God, and that the Spirit of God dwells in you?" (1 Cor.3.16). We are not to have fellowship with the unfruitful works of darkness, but should expose it to the Light in order than it may be not only revealed but made ineffective or destroyed.

Conformity to the world is saying that we like being slaves. The Israelites said similar things when they considered returning to Egypt. Conformity to the world is also stating, voting with our mind, heart and feet that sin is more preferred than a righteous, honorably standing with God. And like the crowd of Jews said concerning Jesus being crucified, "Let his blood be on us and on our children!" (Mat. 27.25). Which invoked a curse on the Jews that manifested during the Nazi rise to power between 1939-45. About 6 million Jews were killed.

God says that this is a crooked and perverse world, but we can shine as lights upon a hill that cannot be hid, even a force for unbelievers to reckon with. Renewal in the mind is necessary to think like Christ---the Spirit of God in us seeks to change our thinking to match up with His thinking; for out of the abundance of the heart the mouth speaks and corresponding actions will follow. But the world-spirit demands the opposite.

A few of the world-spirit reasoning are:

There is no God, Creator, and therefore no Savior called Jesus: Those who believe this atheist's philosophy usual believe in Evolution, that mankind evolved from apes, and when death comes we no longer exist: Hence, no need to be concerned about sin or its consequences: When you're dead, your dead! They believe, until face with death they cry, "Oh God!"

There is no person called Satan, and no demons spirits or devils: The biggest and most convincing lie that the

Father of Lies ever told was to convince people that he doesn't exist. Not believing that there is a personal Devil, demons or fallen angels is calling God a liar, who stated in the Holy Bible that there is such a person as Satan, the Devil. Also, the spirits that rule over the earth remain concealed and unchallenged.

There is no Heaven or Hell; the world is all there is: This is also the atheist's view. No Heaven, no God; no Hell, no Satan or punishment for evil doing. So it doesn't matter how we live if we will cease to exist like the fish and the birds. Rebellion and lawlessness results; people are robbed, raped, killed and the jails and prisons become a revolving door---not to mention the behind the door abuse and perversion that, like mold, thrives in the darkness.

The intellectuals of the world know all the answers to life: This is pride and arrogance to think that human reasoning can solve or answer all situations and circumstances: Then why isn't there a cure for AIDS, Cancer, or even the common cold? People who depend on human reasoning alone are subject to the control of the world spirits who tell us what to think, when and how to think it; it is also an example how people love the darkness more and rather than the Light of Christ's omniscience—His ability to know everything from the Alpha too Omega.

Man made God instead of the opposite: From the time of Abraham the Hebrew, human being had made gods from wood, stone, bronze and even gold. But since Jehovah of the Old Testament made Himself known, the need of manmade gods remained only with those nations that didn't want to worship the true God. True Christianity is about relationship with God; it is not about statues, crucifixes, rosaries, symbols, places, times, ceremonies, holidays or seasons.

The Bible is completely conceived by man: To them, the account of Genesis and the creation of man is false, and the theory of Evolution is the correct explanation of how man and everything got here. But scientists did not know that the ruling spirits salted Darwin's mind to publish this theory throughout the land. Te scientists have not proven their case because they claim that there is an important link in the chain of events missing in Darwin's Theory; but the atheist immediately jumped at the opportunity to prove that the Bible is wrong, and persuaded schools to teach Evolution instead of Genesis.

Religions are all the same: Not even the leaders or followers of these religions believe this statement; they all think that they have the only way! But the majority of nonreligious people believe mostly in themselves. They also think that all the religious paths lead to the same place called different names such as Heaven, Paradise, Nirvana etc. It counters the claim that Jesus made: "I am the Way, the Truth, and the Life; no one comes to the Father but by Me" (Jn. 14.6).

If it could be proven that Jesus is not the only Way to Heaven, then nothing else that He has said can be trusted either. Therefore, Jesus Christ would not be the Savior of the World because He lied like an ordinary human being; and it is also reasonable to assume that His disciples fabricated the other accounts of His miracles, including Him raising from the dead. So, to the world, Christianity becomes equal to the other paths. This too is one of Satan's master strokes of deception---to hide the Life and Person of Jesus Christ from Man.

Satan is as powerful or more powerful than God: This belief became popular with the supernatural movies like: vampires, The Exorcist, Bewitch, I Dream of Genie, Zombies, and Harry Potter movies.

Although witchcraft has been around for ages, and is recorded as being practiced by several individuals in the Old and New Testaments, there is no recorded cases where Satan ever got the best of God or Jesus either. Yes, Satan fought in Heaven to dethrone God and lost; he was cast down to the earth (Rev. 12.7) where he interfered and deceived mortals and made their lives miserable, but he has never overpowered or defeated God in a one-on-one battle.

Satan uses this belief to keep even Christians in line. Christians have authority over Satan and his demons. Christians can heal the sick and cast demons out of people. Therefore, to keep Christians from doing this, Satan uses fear that the demon will enter the Christian to keep them from "laying hands" on the sick and removing evil spirits that likely have caused the sickness or disease. Still others just want to believe that God is not really all-powerful and can be beaten, and in their mind it justifies them not serving Him.

People are not born in sin and need to be redeemed: This is an example of many philosophies rolled into one belief. It amounts to unbelief and calling God a liar, when He said that all have sinned and come short of the glory or expectations of God; it is saying that God or the Holy Trinity is wrong, unfair, non-existent or some kind of control freaks, by not letting everyone live like they want to. It also says that there is no such thing as sin---only human mistakes and errors; that sin is not an issue or a reality on earth or in their lives; also that the Bible and Jesus are fictitious, that they know what is best for themselves and don't need God, if He were real, to do anything for them.

Homosexuals and Lesbians will be in Heaven: Many Christians believe this too. This is the end times when the U.S. Courts are making decisions based upon what the voters want. In the process, Gays and Lesbians have placed their supporters, Gay, Lesbian or Liberals into top political and judicial positions in local, state and government offices. But no matter what the voters, politicians, Supreme Court Justices---or even an Act of Congress---want on Earth, God is the only One who decides who enters into Heaven. God says in His Word: No Gays or Lesbians will be in Heaven (1 Cor. 6.9). And this applies to Gay or Lesbian Bishops, church leaders, choir directors and members of the congregation.

All men are brothers: This too is a lie from the pit of Hell; it was devised to make no distinction between the Christian and everyone else. Unsaved as well as many Christians believe that everyone---including the followers of Islam---is their brother and spiritual equal. But, Christians are new creations, born again into a separate family, rank and classification all by themselves (not even the holy angels share this rank or classification).

Unregenerate man is lost and separated from God because of his sinful, Adamic nature termed Original Sin, and the willful refusal to accept Jesus Christ as his personal Lord and Savior. According to the flesh, Adam, all human beings are genetically linked, but Christians are in God's Family because of the abiding of the Holy Spirit of God in their human spirit; and the unsaved are in Satan's Family because of the absence of the Holy Spirit. "Now if any man have not the Spirit of Christ, he is none of His"---Rom. 8.9.

If it's State Legal, it isn't sin: Again, even Christian fall for this reasoning: Gays and Lesbian can get married in certain states, medical Marijuana has become legal in many states, and is being widely abused, Gambling Casinos are popping up everywhere, prostitution on ranches in Nevada, sex between consenting adults is no longer frowned upon but is an "alternative" to marriage, "no fault" divorce is in many states.

Adult pornography is legal in America; so is alcohol consumption in bars, clubs and homes is also accepted behavior (alcoholism is now considered a disease, though it is self-inflicted).

Even in the decisions on Capital Punishment, several states motivated by popular vote, executed people whom they later discovered were innocent of the crime; so it too needs to be abolished on the grounds of it being state-sanctioned Murder, aggravated by the fallibility and prejudices of human beings.

The Word of God states that all of these things are sin. If God is the same, yesterday and forever (He. 13.8) what was sin in the past remains to be sin in the present and even in the future. No law of man can change God's nature concerning what is or isn't sin; and He cannot change His mind on the matter.

Once Saved, always Saved: This is the belief that Christians cannot lose their Salvation. This is also a satanic lie. It basically states that now that we are Born Again, we can now return to our old ways, old sinful nature and live like the heathens and not lose our Salvation; it also implies that having the Holy Spirit resident in our human spirit that He is trapped and cannot leave our body no matter what; and also indirectly implies that we do not have to have our minds renewed, nor have to spiritually grow, nor listen to the promptings and leadership of the Holy Spirit to do works acceptable to God; neither do we have to fellowship with the Holy Spirit if we don't want to, or work out our own salvation, as the scriptures state in Phil. 2.12.

There is no Hell: **The doctrine of Inclusion:** This is still another lie similar to several secular philosophies. This one was revealed by the ruling spirit to the mind of a well-known Bishop in the Body of Christ (Bishop in name only). It states that there is no Hell and everyone will go to Heaven. This doctrine would not be different from other secular beliefs except it was introduced by prominent Bishop in the Church. However, if everyone is going to Heaven there is no incentive to do the will of God or the right thing. It opens the door for every wicked and hateful spirit to flood the souls and bodies of mankind until man becomes more rebellious, self-centered and evil than most of Satan's demons; and this doctrine is now being spread and accepted by members of the Church! The Holy Bible states "For as many as are led by the Spirit of God, they are the sons of God" ---Rom. 8.14.

Catholics are not Christians. This is another example of how the demonic powers succeeds in dividing to conquer the Body of Christ. Catholics, though having a distinct history, traditions and the Pope as its head, are nonetheless Christians solely based on their repentance of sins and confession of faith in Jesus Christ as the Lord and Savior. They are Christians, sons and daughters of God because of the indwelling of the Holy Spirit, who seals those who are truly saved. This is the worn out belief that one denomination is better or more spiritual than another, when the reality is that each is part of the same Body and has different functions.

Even in modern times, the demonic hierarchy has caused enormous bloodshed between these two denominations of Christianity to fight and even blow up innocent bystanders in such places as Belfast, Northern Ireland. This behavior is not true Christianity, but aggression; politics, and heathen religious conformity such as many non-Christian religions and sects display---the fighting and killing for political, religious, racial or territorial control.

The Catholic denomination will not ordain women into the priesthood, nor are the male priests and female nuns allowed to get married. This is a tremendous area where the demons of deception and sexual perversions have struck down many aspiring priests of the Catholic denomination.

Protestants are not Christians: This similar to the above. Many Catholics believe that they have the only true path of enlightenment, that the Pope is the only person that God speaks to; and though most Catholics don't read their bibles, they are convinced that Protestants do not know the Lord

Jesus like they do; and that the Protestant idea of talking with Jesus without going through the Blessed Mother Mary and the Apostles is futile. In most Catholic churches, the Holy Communion is not served to non-Catholics, because they believe that Protestants are not "full brothers".

A Women cannot be a priest/minister: This is also the Deceivers lie. In this belief the non-Christian religions and atheists laugh, nor do they care which Christian denomination is better. But the lie of the Devil is that God cannot use women, when the Holy Bible clearly states differently.

In the Old Testament, Deborah was a Judge (King and Priest), Anna was a New Testament Prophetess, plus other examples including apostles. Also, many denominations or individual bishops and pastors will not license or ordain woman. This is more than discrimination but a male ego issue. Men who are insecure about themselves feel threatened by the anointing of fasted and praying women, who many times are greatly submissive, available and usable to the Lord more than men, and actually make up the majority of the Body of Christ.

Men also place unnecessary clothing (no slacks etc), "covering" and religious dress codes on women, when they themselves wear what feels comfortable to them. It is unfortunate for the Body of Christ what Christian women go through at the hands of controlling men!

The above list is not exhausting one, but to give a general outline of a few dominant philosophies and belief-systems that are commonly believed by the masses. Many of these belief-systems were conceived by the demonic counsels and introduced either by the territorial ruling spirits to the mind of a several human beings, who later either taught it to others as either scientific theory, reasoning, philosophies or religions; the purpose of which is to enslave, bind, dominate, mislead and keep those who would be separated from the world system from a greater, personal relationship with Christ, the Life.

The fact that many Christians are carnal and still bound by many of the above systems means that Deliverance and Inner Healing is needed in the Church; but the principalities and powers and rulers of the darkness of this age war against this Spirit-led ministry and those "outlaws" who dare to be set free, who also have the nerve to return to the enemy's camp---the world plantation---and convince others to separate from the world system. The Holy Spirit who declares and decrees the Word, Name and Blood of Jesus would that Christians everywhere be set free to worship and serve God in the spirit of holiness.

This book is not a work designed to beat up on the Church, but to demonstrate where we as the Redeemed of the Lord still have some areas to work on. These are areas where we have maintained conformity to the world, and this hinders our spiritual Growth. We as Christians pray and ask God where we are missing it, and why we are not hearing from Him or growing as fast as others around us are. The answer may be that we are still harboring sections of the world foundation that has to be broken up, hauled away, and a new foundation or section thereof to replace it.

Perhaps we are not dead enough to the world around us, meaning, we are still participating in things and going to places where the grace of God doesn't allow us to be there or participate in. The fact that we are sometimes overly concerned about what people think of us when we are obeying the Word of God is a hint that being a man/world pleaser is present.

"Knowing this, that our old man is crucified with Him, that the body of sin might be destroyed, that henceforth we should not serve sin" Rom. 6.6 (KJV).

"I am crucified with Christ; nevertheless I live; yet not I but Christ lives in me; and the life which I now live in the flesh I live by the faith of the Son of God, who loved me, and gave Himself for me"--- Gal. 2.20 (KJV).

Another area to consider: The Battle of Life is not to strengthen or maintain the old man and his wicked behaviors; that entity must be crucified and suffer death; it is the new man, recreated in Christ Jesus who will enjoy and participate in the battle to exist and stay alive to do the work of Christ on earth. As Christians and new creations, if we lose our physical body we are out of here; we are done here as far as witnessing or preaching the Gospel. Therefore, we have to take care of this physical temple with the new creation inside. Make no mistake---we are NOT attempting to doctor-up the old man to make him a new and improved sinner, one smarter, stronger, more clever through psychology and philosophies, but "transforming" him by the renewing of the mind (Heb.11.2).

Apostle Paul stated that crucifying the flesh doesn't involve the actual physical death of the fleshly body; as stated earlier---lose this temple and we are history until Jesus returns with us for the Battle of Armageddon. But the scriptures use the term "reckon" which means consider ourselves dead or unresponsive to the temptations and cohesions to sin, as though the mail came to the wrong address, or we moved and left the Devil no forwarding address!

The body of sin is the desire and predisposed nature of all human beings to love darkness more than the Light of Christ. It is also Adamic sin including generational curses, plus the will of the territorial spirits that govern the region we live under. Remember that the plantation slaves taught their children how to be slaves, not how to be free. And so the children's great expectations was aborted in its infancy, unless a free-spirited person intervened.

This great apostle also stated that though he is crucified (reckoned himself as dead) at the cross of Calvary, he partook and shared in the death of Jesus of Nazareth. Now in the same way that Jesus lives as a resurrected Person who is the Resurrection and the Life of the Resurrection, Christ lives in Paul.

Notes

CHAPTER THREE
SPIRITUAL WICKEDNESS

The Battle of Life also includes maintaining the physical body that Adam was made from in Genesis 1.26. After God made Adam and Eve, He gave them dominion and jurisdiction over the entire physical creation; not only the Garden but the entire Earth, the other planets and the solar system; this jurisdiction included the distant galaxies with their stars (suns) and planets.

Soon after, Lucifer, the chief of the fallen angels, deceived Eve, she in turned persuaded Adam into entering High Treason against God. This was a willful and blatant disregard for God's commandment and Word. They were kicked out the Garden and the Presence and Fatherly protection of the Lord God. (Gen.3.24). At this point Lucifer, not Adam, became the god of the physical universe, of matter, space, energy, human and non-human thoughts; he controls these arenas---but not the Spirit Realm, Trinity, Spiritual Laws or archangels that govern the Godhead and creation.

Soon after Satan assumed legal jurisdiction of the spiritual contract and document of entitlement, his governing hierarchy of the Physical and Psychic Realms began. He set up his command chain in which to effective govern his domain, and dug in to hold onto his ill-gotten prize till the end of time.

"Then the Lord said to Cain, "Why are you angry? Why is your face downcast? If you do what is right, will you not be accepted? But if you do not do what is right, sin is crouching

at your door; it desires to have you, but you must master it"--
- Gen. 4.6 (NIV).

As people began to multiply on the face of the earth, so did Satan's influence and control over them. It soon became increasingly more difficult to stay alive and remain in contact with God. Sin had entered the world and with it arrived the first murder: Cain killed his brother Abel.

Cain was jealous and envious of his brother Abel because Abel was a worshipper of God and chose to obey God's commandments and ordinances. Abel chose to allow his faith to govern his life; but Cain chose human reasoning and emotions to govern his life, a reasoning that was subject to the input, manipulation and persuasion of the ruling spirits of that era. Cain had a humanistic philosophy that opposed the Spiritual Law of Faith; faith being a powerful non-carnal or traditional weapon against Satan and his twisted hordes of demons, sin, sicknesses and diseases.

God, who knows all things, tried to help Cain out of the situation that he was in. Cain had thinking distortions; Cain found it difficult to believe that God meant what He said concerning how and what to sacrifice as an offering for sin. In fact, Cain refused to believe that he was a sinner. His thoughts, feelings and emotions brought him to the conclusion---with the assistance of the demonic rulers---that he was right and God was wrong. And therefore Cain also concluded that he knew what was best for himself, and if God required any type of offering, Cain would give him what he wanted to give Cain offered God fruit and vegetables from the cursed ground that he toiled in each day until exhausted. He believed that it was all God's fault that he and the family, Adam and Eve, had to work so hard when God could have made their lives easier. Cain was aware of how it was in the Garden of Eden. But now he had two burdens to resolve: God and Abel. So he decided to permanently get rid of the one: Abel. This was what the rulers told him to do: Kill righteous Abel!

God explained to Cain that if he followed His commandments all would be well; but if he didn't---sin, Satan and the rulers of the earth were crouching at his door. They waited for him to open the door, then pounce on him, and tear his soul completely away from God, by destroying his spiritual and natural life. This would make him a slave and ambassador of sin, to persuade others to committed more sin and rebellion against God's Word and Name.

The battle to stay alive and the battle to draw near to God continued as people had to daily make choices whether to live by Faith in God or their own self-life, reasoning, decisions and emotions. There was no one to ask directions from, for they were pioneers, living in a world but not of it; there were no tracks to follow, for they had not come this way before.

Noah had Faith, trusted in and believed God's Word. He labored and preached for 150 years that the world was going to end via a great flood, but no one believed him neither did they get saved. The human reasoning of the people concluded that since it had never rained, but only a mist arrived every morning to water the earth, that the likelihood of anything like actual liquid falling from the sky was zero. They dismissed Noah as a lunatic using scare tactics to get them to worship his God. They also believed that he was also a deceived fool for building a cruise ship in the middle of the desert!

But Noah built the arc and saved himself, family and animals. The rain fell from the sky according to the Word of the Lord as spoken by Noah; not according to logic or science. The water flooded the earth for 150 days—one day for every year that the people didn't listen to Noah. The people were destroyed, and the rulers of the darkness had no more servants to manipulate into thinking and acting out their dispositions. But then there were Noah and his family.

Noah had three sons: Shem, Ham and Jepheth. Noah planted a vineyard and got drunk off of the wine. He laid naked in his tent. His son, Ham, saw him and told his brothers. The two brothers didn't look at their father but covered him. When Noah sobered up and found out what Ham had done (perhaps he laughed about what he saw, who knows), he cursed Ham's son who wasn't even born yet (Canaan) and made him a slave (Gen. 9.18-27). Noah's anger concerning his respect, pride and tradition led him to curse members of his own family, to prophesy ill when it was in his power to bless all of his sons and their children's children throughout history. This is what the demonic kingdom seeks.

Years later Abram the Hebrew, a man who chose to walk by Faith and not by sight, was called forth by God out of Ur of the Chaldeans to go to a land that God would later show him. God told him "Leave your country, your people and your father's household...So Abram left, as the Lord had told him; and Lot went with him. He took his wife Sari and all the possessions they had accumulated and the people they had acquired in Haran" (Gen. 12.1-5).

Taking Sari, his wife was within God's pan, but Lot and some of the other people was Abram's insecurity and interpretation of what God said! Soon after a famine came and Abram went down to Egypt to live there for a while. But as he entered Egypt, the lying spirit over that region placed fear in the prophet's heart that God wouldn't or couldn't protect him, and that he needed to lie to everyone and say that Sari was his sister instead of his wife, that if he didn't lie the Egyptians would kill him and take her anyway. So Abram convinced Sari to go along with the lie Gen. 12.10-13).

Here was a lying spirit telling Abram how to live his life; telling him to forget about the promises and protection of God and submit to the natural response to the fear of death. Fortunately for Abram, God is patient, merciful and of great compassion. He rescued Abram, His prophet and Sari from the Egyptian Pharaoh, and from Abram's plan, his mental weakness to outside pressures warring against his faith in God Most High.

Later, Abram's group and Lot's group got a dispute over there not being enough room and grazing land for the two increased families to live close together. So to keep the quarreling down Lot moved down to Sodom. Out of all the places to live, Lot moved into a city that the Lord stated: "Now the men of Sodom were wicked and were sinning greatly against the Lord" (Gen. 13.13).

Sodom and its twin city, Gomorrah, were cities where homosexuals and Lesbians lived and practiced sexual perversions. Logical reasons why Lot would knowingly move to such a place was that he was a homosexual, had homosexual tendencies or the ruling spirits over that territory lured him down there; one visit to that city and conversation with the people and Lot knew what type of people they were. Lot didn't move there thinking that he could change them or live among them regardless of their lifestyle. He went down there hooked like a fish on a strong line, not caring about himself or the souls of his family. He obeyed without question the drawing forth of the territorial ruling spirit.

In the process of time, war broke out between nine kings and kingdoms. Sodom and its allied kings were defeated and overtaken by King Kedorlaomer and his allied kings. Lot and his household and goods were also taken.

When news of Lot taken captive reached Abram, he sprung into action with his household of 318 trained men. His renewed Faith in God catapulted him to heights of genuine courage, leadership and persistence. He pursued with an anticipation and expectation of recovering all that the devil stole from his family. Being vastly outnumbered in the natural, he knew that in the Spiritual Realm that with God at his side, was more than the whole world that could be against him. He already had the victory. Abram and his servants defeated this vast army. He recovered all---more than Lot and his possessions.

The King of Sodom, most likely a homosexual, came out and offered to reward Abram for his success. He knew that in the natural there was no way this side of the grave that Abram could have defeated with only 318 men what the king couldn't do with thousands of trained warriors.

Abram refused to accept his offering: "But Abram said to the king of Sodom, "I have raised my hand to the Lord, God Most High, Creator of heaven and earth, and have taken an oath that I will not accept nothing belonging to you, not even a thread or a thong of a sandal, so that you will never be able to say, "I made Abram rich" (Gen. 14.22-23).

Abram already promised God that if He would help to save Lot, his family and possessions, that he wouldn't receive a reward. But the King of Sodom, working for the demonic authorities, attempted to get Abram to renege on his promise to God and receive a reward for defeating the kings. Abram wanted no part of the tainted spoils of a people that God was ready to destroy. Abram wouldn't accept the cursed objects that would demonically become a detestable object, whereby demons would have a legal right to interfere in his life; he would not receive such gifts from such people who God declared were wicked.

Abram also knew the heart of the King of Sodom. He knew that the purpose of the offer was to brag in the future and say that Abram was rich not because God was with him and made him rich and prosperous, but that the king gave

Abram such a great reward of cattle, servants, gold and silver for his bravery in working for the King of Sodom and their interests.

"Then Melchizedek king of Salem brought out bread and wine. He was the priest of God Most High, 19 and he blessed Abraham, saying, Blessed be Abram by God Most High, Creator of heaven and earth, 20 and blessed be God Most High, who delivered your enemies into your hand. Then Abraham gave him a tenth of everything."

Abram knew where his help came from. He recognized by way of his anointing who Melchizedek was. He was the High Priest of God Most High, the Christ of God, the Eternal High Priest of the Eternal Sanctuary of Heaven. The priest brought bread and wine: The bread represented the broken body of Jesus, the Messiah the Anointed One whom would come; and the wine symbolized the Messiah's shed blood for the forgiveness of sins.

Abram gladly gave Him the tithe, because He was worthy to receive it; whereas, the King of Sodom was merely another sinner needing to repent from his wicked ways. Abram knew that if he would have honored the King of Sodom, then the King of Salem---which means the Prince of Peace, would not have come down from His sanctuary to commune and fellowship with him.

Shortly thereafter, God made the Abrahamic Covenant with Abram, the man who had the Promise of God. God, who by two immutable things---His Word and His Promise, swore that He would never lie or deceive Abram or his descendants; and Abram considered Him faithful who made the promise. God sealed it with His oath, whereas, God was not ashamed to be called the God of Abraham's; nor was Abraham ashamed to claim God as his refuge, strength and exceedingly great reward for generations to come.

That day Abram's name became Abraham, the father of many nations. But while he communed with God, Lot and his family had already moved back to Sodom; and it was business as usual in sin city. After all that Lot had gone through, he moved back into that wicked city.

But God had other plans for Sodom and Gomorrah. The outcry against that city was so great and their sin so grievous that He sent two angel to destroy them. But as God spoke to Abraham, and in order to honor His Covenant with Abraham, said to the destroying angels, "Shall I hide from Abraham what I am about to do? Abraham will become a great and powerful nation, and all nations on earth will be blessed through him" (Gen. 18.17,18). For the Lord would do nothing except He first reveal it to His servants the prophets.

Though Abraham knew what type of people lived in those two cities, God knew that there weren't ten people that he felt were worthy of being spared. Abraham continued to intercede, but even he knew that they were a perverse group of people. Nevertheless, for Abraham's sake and because of his Faith in God, the Lord decided to spare Lot and his family, though the Lord provided no information that He considered Lot and his family worth saving!

The two angels who looked like ordinary men entered Sodom. Lot met them and invited them to stay in his home; but during the night all the young and old men in town surrounded the house and demanded that Lot send the men out because they wanted to rape them. Lot offered his virgin daughters to them but they would have none of it: They were homosexuals. They threatened to treat Lot in a worst manner than the strangers. Thereafter, the angels pulled Lot back into the house and struck down the Sodomites with blindness.

The following day the angels had to grab Lot by the arm because he hesitated to leave Sodom though he knew that it was going to be destroyed. He didn't want to leave the city because the city and its ways were in him; on a daily bases, he was vexed and indoctrinated by the filthy conversations and the oppression of the principalities encouraging the vile behaviors.

They fled to another city called Zoar, and were instructed not to look back at the destruction of Sodom and Gomorrah. They were instructed not to look back at their past but into their future. But Lot's wife, not willing to let go of the past and the familiar, disobeyed the angels and the Word of the Lord: She looked back because she didn't really want to leave the city anymore than Lot did. She risked it all for another glimpse. She turned into a pillar of salt.

"One day the older daughter said to the younger, "Our father is old, and there is no man around here to lie with us as is the custom all over the earth 32 Let's get our father to drink wine and then lie with him and preserve our family line through our father" Gen. 19.31,32 (NIV).

At Lot's pleading with the destroying angels, they allowed him to go to the city of Zoar instead of the mountains. Suddenly gripped by a strange and dreadful fear of the citizens of Zoar, when there was no external evidence that the people of Zoar threatened them, Lot and his daughters were driven by the tormenting spirits from their warm beds, into the rocky mountains. Now they lived in a cave!

But little did they know that although the cities of Sodom and Gomorrah were destroyed, the perversion and wickedness resided inside them. The enemy of their souls set them up for moral failure. They were angry and bent on revenge because God destroyed their cities, but saved Lot and his daughters. So when the Lord and the destroying angels went back to Heaven, the evil territorial spirits plotted to defile and corrupt those whom the Lord saved; they lured them out of a safe city by using fear, then isolated them in a mountain cave for them to live as mere beasts, and host for the iniquity that would follow.

Lot's daughters were previously engaged to husbands but both men didn't believe that the city was going to be destroyed, because Lot didn't have a reputation as a Godly man; he had no testimony or credibility as a reputable prophet or friend of God as his uncle, Abraham the Hebrew did. Both men remained in Sodom and were destroyed with the others. Lot's wife was killed when she looked back. Now Lot's two daughters, motivated by lust and deviant thinking distortions, hatched a plan that to them sounded reasonable.

The Word of God stated that Lot allowed his daughters to get him drunk on two occasions while his daughters had sex with him, but neither time was he aware of what had happened, although his seed was gone out of his body.

The plan of the demonic territorial overseers was to mentally blind Lot to the physical sensations of sexual intercourse; or if he was aware of it, he didn't care about the moral or spiritual consequences, the outworking of sin in his mortal body. The consequences were that both Lot's daughters got pregnant by him.

As time moved on, the demonic kingdom grew stronger and more deviant in their control and manipulation of the thoughts and emotions of the people. Every chance they got, they made life difficult and at times unbearable even for those who wanted to do what was right in the sight of God, yet didn't understand or were insensitive to perceive the influences from above.

Even after Abraham's moment of weakness when he lied to Pharaoh, again faced with the fear of death concerning his wife Sarah, declared to Abimelech, king of Gerar, that she was his sister (Gen. 20.1). One would think that he had learned his lesson that God would protect His servants who love and obey him. But the spirit of fear being such a ruthless and merciless taskmaster, blocked out Abraham's Faith and the desire to stay alive, the self-preservation of the self or soul-life took control of the situation; that part of Abraham that would lie if it benefited him worked against the will and Promise of God for his mortal life.

God spoke to Abimelech in a dream: "You are as good as dead because of the woman you have taken; she is a married woman" (Gen. 20.3). Abimelech couldn't wait to give Abraham his wife back! But he couldn't believe that Abraham would tell such a lie and get him into trouble with God.

He found it difficult to believe that a man and prophet of God would do such a thing to an innocent man. He said in a very hurtful way: "What have you done to us? How have I wronged you that you have brought such guilt upon me and my kingdom? You have done things to me that should not be done" (Gen. 20.9,10). He basically said that because Abraham was a man of God, he held him to a higher standard than others who didn't know God.

But what saved Abimelech was that God knew that the king had been tricked. The Lord prevented Abimelech from having sexual relations with Sarah, and Abraham explained to Abimelech the reason why he did what he did: That he reasoned that the people had no fear of God in them, so he thought it wise and necessary to lie to them!

This was Abraham's thinking distortion---that it was better to lie than die! (Gen.20.11). He was under tremendous pressure by the demonic powers that seized upon another opportunity to ruin his testimony before men, in order to continue their unchallenged authority on the earth; an authority that was easily beaten down and flattened by the Spiritual Law of Faith---if only Abraham and others would stand firm and uses this weapon to demolish demonic influences.

Years later, the promised son of Abraham, Isaac and his wife, Rebekah, were instructed by God to go down to Gera in the land of the Philistines . There was a famine in the land, so God said to Isaac: "Stay in this land for a while, and I will be with you and will bless you" (Gen. 26.1-6).

It so happened that King Ablimelech was there, though this king was likely the son of the other Ablimelech whom Abraham deceived. The men of the land asked him if Rebekah was his wife, and he told them that she was his sister. Rebekah was very beautiful and he was afraid that the men would kill him for her; this was the same influence , the territorial spirit of fear and lying that years earlier pressured his father to forget about his Faith and the protection of God. And though Isaac shared the same promise and protection, he also bowed to the ruling spirit over the area. Fortunate for Isaac and Rebekah, God remained faithful to His promises though they failed to keep up their end of the Covenant.

Territorial spirits remain stationary for hundreds of years; some have ruled certain areas for thousands of years. Still others shift regularly to introduce new distractions, to implement social and judicial changes that are designed to keep us humans under control and sinning until they can arrange for our untimely deaths.

For example: Drugs, riots, incurable diseases, pandemics, wars, acts of terrorism and violent crimes are shifts in the regions. These are but a few of the things that are introduced when territorial spirits shift, or make room for another powerful spirit to introduce new evil into a specific area. The exercise of our persistent Christian Faith and Intercessory prayer becomes the weapons most effective to limit the effectiveness of prince spirits.

The battle of and for Life at times seems like one and the same battle. Adam, Eve, Cain and Abel were the first to experience it; the evil prince spirits were just getting started, setting up their military-style order. Noah, though he wanted to please God in every way, relaxed and before long he was drunk and out of his mind on the wine of the world. Abraham, Sarah, Lot and then Isaac and Rebekah feared the spirits ruling the times, who told mankind what to think and how to think it. Then came Jacob who was a trickster, liar and deceiver, who one day wrestled with God---lost, and was changed for the better forever. And though his treacherous offspring sold Joseph into Egyptian slavery (Gen. 37), their evil intent was turned into God's good to save the Nation of Israel.

Yes, these were difficult times on the earth. A time when mankind didn't have the Holy Spirit inside to help, though many Israeli prophets, priests and kings had God's mantle, the Anointing upon them like a garment. And this didn't make them immune to the powers that ruled, but gave them help in the battle of life.

"And Satan stood up against Israel, and provoked David to number Israel. 3 But King Solomon loved many strange women....3 he had seven hundred wives, princesses, and three hundred concubines, and his wives turned away his heart"---1 Chron. 21.1 1 Kgs. 11.1,3 (KJV).

The first time that the name Satan is used in the Holy Bible is concerning the god of this world directly influencing King David to disobey God's commandment not to number Israel. David was forbidden to count how many fighting men he had in the army, but by Faith was to depend on God to deliver Israel's enemies into their hands. By inciting David to number Israel, it inflated David's ego to deceive him into believing that it wasn't the Lord who fought Israel's battles and brought them victories, but the mighty men of valor. Satan personally handled this matter because Israel was

God's land army fighting against Satan's land armies in the region. So, to get the upper hand, Satan puffed David up like a birthday balloon and convinced David to sin against God.

Satan and the territorial spirits had already corrupted King Saul, the former King of Israel. They caused the king to disobey God's commandments and unlawfully sacrifice animals unto the Lord, which was the duty of a priest. Saul also hunted David through the mountains, valleys and swamps like David was a rabid wolf. When the demons were done with Saul, he fell on his sword and committed suicide.

This was because the Rulers of the Darkness knew that David was anointed and appointed by God to be the next king of Israel. And when David killed Goliath the Philistine, their instrument of fear on earth, their attention was directed towards destroying David, the man that God said was after His own heart. David was a man who knew the heart of God and was willing to be led by Him.

One day when David should have been at the battle, instead he was at home. Suddenly, he arose from bed and went up on the roof. There at a distance he saw a lovely woman as she bathed; her name was Bathsheba. David's flesh got the best of him; he sent for Bathsheba and then committed adultery with her (2 Sam. 11.2). She got pregnant, and to cover up that sin he had her husband Uriah killed. This sort of reasoning and conduct was not typical of David, who was a handsome and compassionate man who could have had any single woman that he wanted. He also was a poet and psalmist.

David was set up. It was not like him to spawn such an evil plan. He was minding his own business when suddenly he had an urge to go up on the roof! And why was this woman bathing in the open? Then David tried his best to get Uriah to have sex with his wife as to blame the pregnancy on Uriah. When this failed, David gave Uriah a sealed note to carry to the captain, a note that spelled out how Uriah was to be killed in battle as to make him look like a casualty of war!

Familiar spirits---spirits assigned by Satan to David at birth---watched him closely, his every move, and listen to his words in order to discover what manner of sins David liked, and in turn the evil spirit set him up; and even provided the right beauty, trimmings and enticements that set David's soul on fire with lust.

Other spirits later brought forth the outworking of his lust for women; the generational curses attached themselves to David's bloodline.

Years later, David's son Ammon raped Tamar, his sister; both were victims of the curse; then Absalom murdered Ammon; like David murdered Uriah. Years later Absalom usurped David's God-given authority as king of Israel, and forced David and those loyal to him to flee for their lives. Then a tent was pitched on the roof (probably the same roof that David saw Bathsheba) and Absalom had sexual intercourse with David's Concubines in the sight of all Israel (2 Sam. 16.22).

Later, King David's son, King Solomon was not only overcome by the same spirits of sexual sins, but his thousand women and the idolatry spirits that inhabited them persuaded the wisest man that has ever lived---a genius who built the marvelous Temple in Jerusalem---to not only build his women heathen places of worship, but Solomon bent his knees in submissive worship. He also stopped serving the Lord God of Israel, and causes the whole of Israel to fall into idol worship; Solomon worshipped the demons that were now unchallenged and comfortably seated in the atmosphere above Israel.

"The LORD said to Satan, Where have you come from? Satan answered the LORD, "From roaming through the earth and going back and forth in it."---Job 1.7,8 (NIV).

When the Lord called a meeting of those who are in authority, Satan attended the meeting: He is the god of the Physical Universe. Nowhere in scripture is this disputed, but instead verified. The Lord asked him basically what he had been doing, and the answer was simple: Patrolling his dominion to see that everything and everyone is doing what he wants them to do.

God also asked him did he know Job. And the answer came back that he had been after Job for some time, but couldn't corrupt Job because God had a hedge around him. But this was only because Job prayed daily, repented of sins, prayed for his family, and had utmost faith in God. Job utilized the Spiritual Law of Faith; that is why Satan couldn't touch Job. Job realized the power of fasting, prayer, praise, worship and fellowship with the Spirit. So Satan had to get God's permission to harm Job.

Notes

CHAPTER FOUR
FAITH COUNTED AS RIGHTEOUSNESS

"For therein is the righteousness of God revealed from faith to faith; as it is written, The just shall live by faith"--- Rom. 1.16 (KJV).

The moment that God said to Adam, "do not" any particular thing, it also opened the door for Satan, who is the prince of rebellion, to exercise power and influence over those who oppose God's Word. Satan's authority over human beings only exist because we as human beings do the opposite of what God says to do; his other authority exist over the fallen angels/demons. When we align our thoughts, actions and hopes with the god of this world, we will reap what he (and we) sows. And when thoughts become actions and actions are repeated, they became second nature, and thus a habit or addiction is born.

From Adam to the church of today, the desire to do what's right may be there but the power to put it into practice was and still is lacking in many of our lives. There are several scriptural reason for this: How can great men like Adam, Noah, Abraham, Isaac, David, Solomon and many others fall prey to Satan and his influences? Why is sin reigning as king in our lives?

After Adam, who had the first Covenant of Faith (the Dispensation of Innocence), lost his kingdom and also his high spiritual status, God had to again reconstitute the principles of Faith into Adam's heart so that he could not only fellowship with Him but protect himself in the new world order. Satan set up his initial government, but was digging in for a long drawn-out battle with God over the souls of human beings; these were spirit-beings made in God's image and likeness that Satan wants to capture and make forever his servants.

God separated Abraham (the Dispensation of Faith) and made the second Covenant of Faith; believing God's Word was counted as faith and righteousness. But when the children of Israel, former Egyptian slaves, but free moral agents, didn't want to, or were not psychologically sensitive and alert to believe God or His Word, the Law (Dispensation of Law) was handed down to Moses. Israel, though free from physical slavery, were still bound by the slave mentality---the evil genius and his indoctrination---and couldn't believe God's words, to have their Faith counted as righteousness, whereas, they too would be friends of God.

The Law of Moses, rather, the Law of Sin and Death, like a mirror shows the face of the person looking into it (being judged and examined by its standards), and exposes the sinful character and behavior flaws of that person; but the Law has no power to change anyone, only convict of sin without mercy or partiality; and so Satan also used the Law to inflict condemnation, guilt, shame, hopelessness, inferiority and other controlling influences.

"Because that when they knew God, they glorified Him not as God, neither were thankful; but became vain in their imaginations, and their foolish hearts were darkened. 22 Professing themselves to be wise, they became fools" --- Rom. 1.21,22. That sums up the end results of Satan's worldly indoctrinations.

The people in the Old Testament thought no differently than many do today; the masses think that they are really free---because the Constitution states it in writing---but freedom to them means not answering to God's Word. They enjoy living free from the commandments and oversight of God, when in fact they are sinners, spiritual fugitives from

God and slaves of the prince of darkness. They reason, like their predecessors and are convinced by the same demonic rulers that they can rob, swindle, lie, steal, rape, fornicate, murder, be homosexuals and Lesbians---and there would be no consequences from God.

Finally, though God is longsuffering and patient, as He shut the door on the condemned world in the days of Noah and the flood; and it didn't matter how much the people begged, wailed and promised to change, God didn't open the door of the arc and let them in---so will the time come to pay up and shut up!

"And even as they did not like to retain God in their knowledge, God gave them over to a reprobate mind, to do those things which are not convenient"---Rom. 1.28). They didn't desire to get to know God; they didn't think that God was worth knowing. Nothing has changed. The same spirit operates today in what the Bible terms, "the spirit that works in the hearts of the children of disobedience."

There comes a time when God says enough is enough! Those who profess that they have all the answers and don't need God, will one day be looking into the hateful eyes of their master---Satan. God will give up and let them do what they want to do---act out their depraved imaginations and fantasies until they smell the burning brimstone and see the blue flames of fire in the pits of Hell.

But all is not lost! There is forgiveness of sin through Jesus Christ, the Messiah. There is righteousness apart from the Law, and it is entirely by Faith in Jesus Christ. There is no other Name given to us whereby we must be Saved!

The Law was a legal instrument and document, an indictment against mankind: "For all have sinned and come short of the glory of God" (Rom. 2.23). A higher Law, the Law of the Spirit of Life was implemented that all could be declared righteous---justified---declared "Not Guilty" and set free of the Law of Sin and Death (and the eternal Death Penalty), though Jesus Christ our Lord.

Abraham was justified by Faith before the Law was given to Moses; his works, both good and bad, were not considered in this legal action; and later on, the Jews were **justified by Faith** and the Gentiles **justified through Faith** in Jesus Christ (Rom. 3.30). Yet, the Law is not done away with but remains intact for those who do not have Faith in Jesus Christ, those following cults and religions.

It often angers people when they hear that we Christians claim forgiveness of sins by two simple acts called repentances and Faith in Jesus Christ. What kind of God, they say, would justify the wicked? The answer: A good God! Yes, it's true, through Jesus Christ our former and future sins were dealt with over two thousand years ago at the cross of Calvary. We are blessed to have our sins forgiven, our iniquities covered by the shed Blood of Jesus.

And the promise that God made to Abraham that he would be the heir of the world, was not to him or his seed through the Law but through Jesus Christ, the Seed, and the righteousness of Faith. Now we have peace with God and within, and immediate access to grace, mercy, love and the glory of God. Even in the days when we didn't have strength to come to God because of the evil influences above and around us---Christ has already died for us, to bring us to this point in the Battle for Life.

When we were His enemies and doing everything that we were insane and devious enough to do, we were reconciled to God the Father by the death of Jesus Christ, how much more are we reconciled by the Eternal Life of Jesus Christ, who is the propitiation (substitute) for our sins. For it was the goodness of God that led us to repentance (Rom. 2.4).

It is through the Spiritual Law of Faith that we are free from the tyranny of evil spiritual rulers. Being Justified by Faith, we are also free from the Law of Sin and Death, free from addictions, free from habitual personal sins that have become a ball and chain, binding us to serve Satan all the days of our life---then die and be his subjects in Hell too? We cannot afford to let sin reign as king over us.

"Knowing this, that our old man is crucified with him, that the body of sin might be destroyed, that henceforth we should not serve sin"---Rom. 6.6(KJV).

We as Christians are seated together with Him at the throne of God. We are in Him (Father, Son/Church, Holy Ghost). We are baptized into Jesus Christ and adopted via the action of the Holy Spirit into the Family of God. But in order for us to be seated and baptized into Him, we had to also die with Him. And by this understanding, we reckon (consider as fact and act upon it) ourselves to be dead (unresponsive) to sin (in the same way a physically dead person doesn't respond when spoken to, insulted or threatened).

So when the Tempter comes to persuade us to sin we do not respond at all. We are also buried with Him in baptism into death, and in the same manner and verbal commandment that the Father exerted His Faith and power when He raised Jesus from the dead, we too are raised up by the commandment and glory of God to a new Life without sin.

Apostle Paul wrote in Romans about the old man being crucified with Christ, yet lives on, but not the old man but Christ within us is alive; and He has no interest or inclination in sinning or serving the Devil. The body of sin is the human body and its manners and customs laboring under the Law of Sin and Death. Without the Holy Spirit, the body and soul is but a pawn in the hand of the wicked one; the body and soul is a dead man walking---a spiritually dead entity who is only a shell and soul housing the true person, the human spirit.

Being free from being a servant to sin makes us free and available to be used of God. "For the wages of sin is death; but the gift of God is eternal life through Jesus Christ our Lord" (Rom. 6.23). Only an insane or demonized person would elect to go to Hell. Death, by its very nature, is not the type of reward that any sane person would want as payment for services. A gift from God of Eternal Life is more fitting a reward for our praise, worship and service to God.

The Law was and is an instrument that God uses to teach the principles of obedience and Faith. As said earlier, the unsaved, cults and religions are under the Law of Sin and Death. But as Apostle Paul stated, that which was meant by God to bring Israel to repentance and Faith, Satan corrupted and sent spirits of guilt, shame, worthlessness, helplessness, abandonment and fear of death to torment Israel their entire lifetime; and this keep them in bondage.

Today, Satan uses the same legal strategies when dealing with the Law to keep us believing that we are not worthy to have God in our lives, or are too bad a sinner, or completely deceives us into following another religious path that promises the same results as Christ; until we take our last breath, and the demons from Hell come to our bedside to drag us to Hell and the pit!

Paul stated that there was a struggle within: "I do not understand what I do. For what I want to do I do not do, but what I hate I do. 16 And if I do what I do not want to do, I agree that the Law is good. 17 As it is, it is no longer I myself that do it, but it is sin living in me" (Rom. 7.15-17).

This has been the dilemma of many Believers and unbelievers. How it is that we can want to do the right thing but wind up doing the wrong thing? Paul said that when he wanted to do good, evil was right there with him. He saw another law at work in his members waging war against the law of his mind and making him a prisoner of the Law of Sin and Death:

This opposition is the Battle for (Eternal) Life being waged not outside but inside us. Evil meaning some power or influence exerting or putting pressure on us to do opposite of what is right in working out our own salvation.

Paul claimed that he was a wretched man, and many times we feel the same way when we have a setback as we Battle for Life and fail to give God our best. Paul cried out to be rescued from this body of death. He realized and now we also know that through Jesus Christ help is on the way!

The battlefield takes place in our minds but the enticements, temptations, philosophies and religions are outside of us. The same five senses we have: Sight, smell, hearing, taste and touch, are the same five senses that the prince of this world and his operatives use to contact and communicate their will to our conscious brain. But he also has another avenue of attack, and that is through the subconscious brain. He often communicates with us while we are asleep---even sends false visions and recurring past sinful acts that we have committed, in order to keep us bound to our past mistakes and sins, or get us interested in returning to our past sinful behaviors; he most often appeals to our pleasure principle, and our desire to be loved and respected by family and society.

When the Holy Spirit moved us to repent of our sins and accept Jesus Christ as our personal Lord and Savior, a dramatic shift too place inside us. We received the Holy Spirit and our human spirit was awakened and (Christ)"made us sit together in heavenly places in Christ Jesus" (Eph. 2.6).

We gave all that we have control of to Jesus Christ the moment we accepted Salvation. But at best we only have control of 90% of our entire heart, and the other 10% is still corrupted by the world and belongs to us, the flesh nature; the self-life that was in control up to the point we accepted Jesus Christ, did not agree with the rest of us because it didn't want to, and still doesn't want to stop sinning, neither does it really want to serve God.

Now, the Law of sin and Death will work with the part of us that refuses the Salvation that Jesus died for; it will, with the negative assistance of the world rulers and those human beings loyal to them, strive to win back the throne of the self; the old man wants a comeback! He is secretly running covert schemes, operations and assignments deep in the sub-conscious mind. Even when we are asleep, the subconscious mind is being used by the self-life, the old unregenerate man, to topple the reign of Christ in our lives.

For example: When Israel grew tired of fighting the "ites" and failed to utterly destroy them as God instructed: To literally kill them, not wound them so that they would recover. Because they failed to destroy and completely drive out the enemy, the few that were left multiplied, and years later King Saul and King David spent most of their lifetimes in full-scale wars with the Philistines and their allies.

Another example is modern medicine: If we have an infection and don't take an antibiotic until the virus is completely destroyed, but stop taking the medicine---not only will the virus return, but will be resistant to the same antibiotic, and we could possibly be worst off then at first!

The part of every Christian---and we are still human and have weaknesses---a part of us that is not completely (reckoned) dead, and is still trying to call the shots (being the former shot-caller for so many years). And what also makes it difficult to keep the old man under, is the power that the old man receives from the Law of Sin and death, the world rulers, demon-inspired philosophies, religions and world reasoning.

The world rulers desensitize us to important Godly issues of morality: Many video games encourage children to be insensitive and ignore moral values and the sanctity of human life by encouraging them to cut off people's heads and limbs; and to machinegun others to death; the reward is to amass huge points---enough to reach the next level of atrocities---which involves the mass murder of "suspected" criminals or terrorists; these are virtual images in the likeness of human beings who are not entitled to a trial or hearing but executed without justice, mercy or hesitation, and all because it's what's expected of the child game player, who has this godlike power because his finger is on the trigger.

The message is that certain people should not be allowed to live; and once the decision is made on who they are, the assignment is to be carried out without question. And there will be a time when the principalities will again target Christians, like it was done in ancient Jerusalem and in Rome.

THE HOLY SPIRIT

"So too the {Holy} Spirit comes to our aid and bears us up in our weakness; for we do not know what prayer to offer nor how to offer it worthily as we ought, but the Spirit Himself goes to meet our supplication and pleads in our behalf with unspeakable yearnings and groaning too deep for utterance"---Ro. 8.26 (Amp. Bible).

Apostle Paul discovered: "I find then a Law, that, when I would do good, evil is present with me" (Rom 7.21). That statement sounds so terrible and haunting; and for the unsaved, rightly so. But we who have received the indwelling of the Person of the Holy Spirit, the third member of the Trinity, have another Law working to help us win the Battle for Life. It is called the Law of the Spirit of Life that is in Christ Jesus.

Through the Law of the Spirit, there is no condemnation, no judgment, and the arrest warrant is cancelled for those of us who have been translated into Christ Jesus, who no longer walk as the unregenerate, spiritually dead but are led, walk, live in the Spirit and newness of life.

We are therefore free from the Law of Sin and Death, the consequences and penalties of sin (but not immune to the out-working of another Spiritual Law called the Law of Reciprocity---sowing and reaping) as long as we do not rely on the animal nature and connection that the flesh has with the world rulers, but rely on the Spirit of God; then the righteous nature of the Law will be fulfilled in us. This is because in the flesh we cannot please God and our best works on our best days are but rotten, filthy rags, grave clothes and smells in His nostrils.

The Holy Spirit when given His course of action will heal and preserve our physical bodies to provide us with a long life and spiritual service that is acceptable to God our Father. For the true sons and daughters of God are those who are led by His Spirit; if we don't have His Spirit resident in us, God does not claim or accepts us into His Divine Family; because we are considered a tare (weed) among the precious grain, or goats that are driven but cannot be led.

It is also the assignment and pleasure of the Holy Spirit to bear witness with our human spirit that we are the children of God. He tells us that we are heirs of God, joint heirs with Jesus Christ.

When the Holy Spirit enters our human spirit, our spirit recognizes Him and cries out Abba---Father. Our human spirit knows who its Father is, and for the first time since we exited our mother's womb the spirit within us feels adequate, loved and secure; before it was unconscious, comatose, unresponsive, collapsed upon itself and useless as far as assisting the soul and body in the Battle of and for Life; but Christ crucified changed that forever.

The whole creation groans and travails like a woman having a baby, while waiting for the sons of God to be revealed; creation is waiting for us, the Earthbound Church to get it together, do what God says, walk and live in the Spirit, so Jesus can come back to take us home. On that day will be the complete redemption of our bodies; we will receive the completion of our Salvation---what has not yet been worked out by and through the Agency of the Holy Spirit in conjunction with our participation and cooperation in the Word of God.

Glorification Day marks the end of the Sanctification Process, the end of the process that the Holy Spirit uses to renew our minds, cleanse us of sin and bad habits. On this day the Church will be presented to Jesus Christ by the Father as a chaste Bride, holy, obedient to her Husband and without spot or blemish.

Sometimes we know that something inside is wrong; we struggle to do what the Word of God says but wind up doing the opposite; it is no longer us, our will being done but the old man using the Law of Sin and Death to have his way, to mount a coup and by force and violence take his throne back. The old man is like the "ites" that multiplied and almost ran Israel back out of the Promised Land.

But fortunate for us, the Holy Spirit monitors the rest of us from His living quarters in our human spirit. He sees the schemes of the flesh and the demonic host, and moves us to pray in the Spirit, in other tongues, as He makes inter-cessions, definite and accurate petitions to the Father. He does this because we do not know how or what to pray for, nor do we know what the demonic scheme is, how, where, day or hour it will transpire.

God who monitors His own Spirit at all times, whether inside Himself or inside us, knows what the Holy Spirit thinks and feels at all times, as the Holy Spirit represents our welfare and the plans, purposes and pursuits of God.

THE SPIRIT OF LIFE

"For the Law of the Spirit of Life in Christ Jesus hath made me free from the Law of Sin and Death"--- Ro. 8.2 (KJV).

The Law of the Spirit of Life is the highest law of God. It is the cohesive element, the Agape Love that binds the Trinity into one unity, moving as three-in-one but separate in personality and function; each Person regarding the other as Himself duplicated, and the Law of the Spirit of Life sustaining them all. As the Holy Spirit of God is the Life that keeps God alive, and makes Him eternal, so this same Spirit residing in us, is effective and active by Faith.

This Law of the Spirit is more than a conquer against the Law of Sin and Death. If God hadn't given us His Spirit by way of the obedience, death and resurrection of Jesus Christ, the entire human population of the world would have been destroyed like Sodom and Gomorrah; for when the stroke of punishment was due, God's wrath and righteous judgment fell full force upon Jesus.

God declared in times past that the wages of sin is death. Jesus Christ received the blow, the punishment for our sins; then on the day of Pentecost (Acts. 2.1) the Holy Spirit entered the world as the direct results of the Promise of the Father; with His entrance and indwelling came the authority of the Law of the Spirit of Life, to cancel the requirements of the Law of Sin and Death.

So as we walk in the Spirit we will not fulfill the lust of the flesh; and if we are willing to be led by the Spirit we are no longer under the Law of Sin but under Grace. It is our choice, because the Law of Sin is not done away with if we choice to walk in it, neither is sin done away with if we chose to continue to sin and live a sinful lifestyle. But to those of us who have reckoned ourselves dead to sin and its consequences, then the Law of the Spirit operates in us.

Many Christians religiously adhere to the notion that once Saved they can go back to their former sinful behaviors and that Grace will automatically cover them; this is called by many "cheap grace"; it is also presumptuous, premeditated sin, a thinking distortion spirit, to believe that either we will repent later or that Grace will automatically cover us; it is also putting God to a foolish test.

Cheapening God's grace is a subtle, dangerous reasoning, the splitting of hairs, a perceived loop hole or grey area that promotes risky behaviors; it causes us to frustrate the Grace of God and try God's patience; this is also the reasoning that many former and present day preachers have moral difficulties, but continue to preach and live sinful and often illegal lifestyles (theft and sexual offences) up to the day they are prosecuted and/or publicly exposed.

For these preachers have forgotten the Word: "Be not deceived God is not mocked: for whatever a man sows, that shall he also reap. For he that sows to his flesh shall of the flesh reap corruption; but he that sows to the Spirit shall of the Spirit reap Life everlasting" ---Gal. 6.8,9).

The Law of the Spirit of Life, through the blessed Lord Jesus Christ, has blessed us on earth with spiritual blessings in heavenly places in Christ. Christ chose us to be a member of His Christian Family before the foundation of the world. He chose us and separated us from the masses to be a holy people. He also elected, predestinated and called us by His

Grace through wisdom and prudence; and forgave us of our sins in order to express His compassion and Love during the dispensations of times, with His spiritual children. He also left us an inheritance and a divine purpose-driven life, as He worked out all situations and circumstances from the end of time backwards to the beginning of time, according to the counsel of His own will.

Those of us who trust in Jesus Christ, are sealed by the Holy Spirit; He is God's down payment and Promise that He will return and finalize the transaction of the purchased possession. Until then, we are to be led by the Spirit with the knowledge that we are in this world but not of it, that we are strangers and foreigners just passing through and not obligated or compelled to make our home here, under the watchful stare of the demonic spirits; but are to keep our eyes on the prize: The One who loves us and gave His life for us.

The Lord Jesus Christ has been made unto us Wisdom and spiritual insight. We experience and are in awe of the "exceeding greatness of His power to us that believe, according to the working of His mighty power, which He wrought in Christ, when He raised Him from the dead, and set Him at His own right hand in the heavenly places. Even when we were dead in sins, He has quickened us **together** with Christ (by grace you are saved) And has raised us up **together**, and made us sit **together** in heavenly places in Jesus Christ" (Eph. 1.19,20;2.5,6).

As the Father, Son, Holy Spirit sit "together" in One unity, so are we seated **together** in them. We are His workmanship, the fruit of His labor in the vineyard, the multiplied single Seed that fell to the earth and died, was buried and produced a multitude of spiritual offspring called Christians. He also planned and predestinated paths for us to walk in to fulfill His purpose and our appointed destinies which includes the Calling and Commission of Ministry Gifts.

Therefore, Jesus Christ is the Prince of Peace; He by the Holy Spirit placed our hand in God's hand so that we walk together in agreement. God in turn cancelled the indictment and spiritual warrant that was pending against us, because Christ has ripped in half the veil that separated us from God because of our sinfulness; and in so doing Christ reconciled us to God by defeating Satan and his not so subtle manipulation of the Law of Sin and Death against us, and thus Christ created a New Creature: A species of being that had never existed before in Heaven or on earth: A Christian.

Therefore the Spirit of Life is the foundation of God, who makes us a habitation of God through the Spirit; a building whose foundation rest upon and are built up on the apostles and prophets, Jesus Christ being the Chief Cornerstone; and because of this we are "strengthened with might by His Spirit in the inner man; that Christ may dwell in your hearts by faith; that ye, being rooted and grounded in love" (Eph. 316,17), may know the Person of Jesus Christ.

Through the Spirit we are not only rooted and grounded in the Love of Christ, but He also gave Ministry Gifts to the Church: Apostles, prophets, evangelists, pastors and teachers for the maintaining and building up of the Body of Christ, until everyone is strong in the Lord and in the power of His might; we are no longer tossed to and fro by human or demonic doctrines, religions or philosophies, or the pleasures of the flesh. "For ye are dead, and your life is hid with Christ in God" (Col. 3.3).

15 "Do not love or cherish the world or the things that are in the world. If anyone loves the world, love for the Father is not in him. 16 For all that is in the world---the lust of the flesh {cravings for sensual gratification} and the lust of the eyes {greedy longings of the mind} and the pride of life {assurance in one's own resources or in the stability of earthly things}---these do not come from the Father but are from the world {itself}"---1Jn. 2.15,16 (Amp. Bible).

Many Christians observe with dismay, "I don't feel dead; I am very much alive and sin every now and then!" The Scriptures do not say that when we receive Salvation and the Holy Spirit indwells us that we immediately stop sinning; if this were the case, 1 John 1.9 would make no sense: "If we confess our sins, He is faithful and just and will forgive us our sins and purify us from all unrighteousness." This verse was written to the Christian Churches---not the local tavern. However, in our Christian life there should be a gradual decrease in sin as we mature in Christ. If there is no decrease in sin due to the renewing of the mind by the Holy Spirit, it is likely that we are no converted, but have a religious or emotional experience, a mental assent to the truth of the Gospel, but no actual heart acceptance and conversion; we need to search the Scriptures.

The Apostle John further declared the Gospel according to what he and the other apostles saw with their eyes, heard with their ears, and participated in the Word of Life, who is Jesus Christ. He touched Jesus, the Word of God, and He is a real Person; and this Eternal Life provided John and the other apostles with fellowship with the Father, Jehovah-Elohim.

John proclaimed that God is Light and there is no darkness in Him. John stated earlier that in Jesus Christ was Life and the Life was the Light of the world. So in the same way that there is no darkness or wickedness in Christ, the ideal lifestyle is there be no wickedness in us, no running errands for the Devil either!

If we walk in the Life and Light of Christ we truly have fellowship with Him, and our Spiritual Gifts and Fruit of the Spirit reflect the authority, personality and character of Jesus Christ, whose Blood already cleansed us from all sins, so all we have to do is accept this as fact and not theory (doubt /unbelief) then live according to it, reckon ourselves already dead to sin but alive in Christ.

To say that we are Christians and love the Life/Light and don't do what the Word says is being a liar, hypocrite and living in the darkness, a shady and shallow existence influenced by this evil world; and those who say that they love Christ but hate others are liars too (1 Jn. 2.9). Liars do not go to Heaven.

John further instructed that the world and everything in it is not to be loved. He is not referring to the people of the world which we should love spiritually and unconditionally. All of us can easily think of someone we do not particularly like and therefore fail to love them; but the love of the world produces dependency on the world which leads to bondage and slavery by those who control the world operations, economy, laws, morals and acceptable behaviors.

As stated in a previous chapter, what may be state, Supreme Court legal or acceptable behavior to society could be blatant sin in the eyes of God.

John stated that those who love the world, the love of the Father isn't in them. So we can conclude that there is another spirit present at work in them taking the place of the Holy Spirit and leading them to love the material rather than the spiritual, the idols (like money) instead of Jehovah (Jesus).

John also called this lying, controlling, worldly spirit the "antichrist" spirit: "Who is a liar but he that denies that Jesus is the Christ? He is antichrist, that denies the Father and the Son" (1 Jn. 2.22). There are many religions and societies that deny that Jesus is the Christ; the world is bursting with religious people.

The key to understanding the mind and heart of God is this: God is Love; not that He only has Love as an attribute flowing out of Him, but that He is "pure" Agape Love. The Apostle John was a man who tapped into this reality, and out of all the Apostles of the Lamb, he laid his head on Jesus' chest in order to be close to His heartbeat, the heartbeat of Love in human form.

He later wrote in 1 Jn. 3.1, "Behold what manner of Love the Father has bestowed upon us, that we should be called the sons of God: therefore the world knows us not, because it knew Him not. Because the world cannot actually know (appropriate or comprehend) the Agape Love of Christ, they are limited to the Phileo (brotherly) and Eros (romantic and sexual) loves that all human beings possess and to various degrees express one to another.

These types of love are often distorted according to individual motive, belief and customs; human loves are also distorted by the territorial spirits who use them to deceive, manipulate, control or precipitate sexual immorality and lust.

But we who have within us Agape Love are being purified on the inside, to produce godly authority, personality and behaviors on the outside. We who are born of God do not habitually sin; we do not practice sin as a lifestyle, but when we discover or are convicted (not found guilty or condemned) by the Holy Spirit that we have sinned, fall on the grace and mercy of God and repent: Confess the sin according to 1 Jn. 1.9, and by faith believe that God is true to His Word and Promise to forgive the sin and to cleanse, and thus bringing us back into right relationship with Him.

The Son of God incarnated into this world specifically to destroy the works of Satan. And in so doing He established who are the children of God, the redeemed of the Lord, from the children of Satan, the children of disobedience.

Cain killed Abel because he didn't love him; and so if we hate our neighbors than we are no better than Cain, because we murdered in our hearts or assassinated their character with our mouth, by denying them our love. We know that we have passed from spiritual death unto Eternal Life, because we unconditionally Love our neighbors and Christian brethren (1 Jn. 3.14,15). And this Agape Love, the Presence of the Holy Spirit in us is greater than the territorial and other evil spirits that are in the world.

Therefore, knowing that we have Agape Love dwelling in us, we ought to love others, and bring them to the level of revelation that we are operating at. Without the God kind of Love, we are no different than the other religions, and no one will see any difference in the way we act than the others--- who have human love too. Agape Love demonstrates by godly works the outworking of the Person with us; whereby our confession penetrates the heart of the listener because the Spirit of God bears witness in them that we are ambassador of God, representing and speaking to them in His behalf. People are searching for love not just another religion, philosophy or a rule book to live by. They are searching for relationship.

God's Love for the lost people of the world is why He sent forth His Son.

FATHER, SON/CHURCH, HOLY SPIRIT

6 "Jesus said unto him, I Am the Way, the Truth, and the Life; no man comes unto the Father, but by Me. 10 I Am in the Father, and the Father in Me..."---John 14.6, 10 (KJV).

These were the words of the Savior of the World as He approached the end of His three and a half years of human ministry. Having loved those who were in the world He loved them to the end. Years of walking the dusty trails of Israel and her neighboring countries was coming to an end; he taught in the synagogues and told the people that the Spirit of the Lord God was upon Him, for He had anointed Him to preach, teach, heal the sick, cast out demons; but above all this---to prepare a people for the LORD, Jehovah-Elohim, the Father and Creator.

The Name (reputation) of Jehovah-Elohim was known by many of the Jewish people in Jesus' earthly pilgrimage; the works of the Holy Ghost was also known by them too; but they didn't personally know the Love of Christ.

So Jesus, the Christ trudged through the Earth Realm to educate and bless them by revealing to them that He was the Word (Christ) whom God created the worlds through, and without Him was not anything made that was made. That God so loved the world that He sent His only begotten Son, so that whosoever believes in Him would not perish, but have everlasting Life, and participate in the Marriage Supper of the Lamb of God.

Jesus proclaimed that He and Jehovah-Elohim are One. This was a truth that many found hard to believe and even offensive, since Jesus of Nazareth obviously looked like a man. He made many bold statements to the intent that people would believe on Him.

Another statement was, "I Am the Way, the Truth and the Life...." He wasn't saying that He was a way, a truth, a life; but He was the only Way, the only Truth, and the only Life; no one could even talk to or ascend to Jehovah-Elohim the Father without going through Christ, the Son.

Jesus told them that God didn't have a son in the way that human beings have children; in eternity before all time He was not the Son of God. At that point He was the Word (Christ) and was with God and the Holy Spirit; when the Word became a human being is when the Father had His Son, born of the virgin Mary.

But now it was time to leave this world, whereby the Ministry of the third member of the Trinity could begin: The Holy Spirit. He told them that He would ask the Father to send another Comforter, the Holy Spirit to abide with them and be in them forever, to such as are truly Saved and endure to the end.

In the Old Testament, the Holy Spirit was the same Person (s) who gloriously dwelled in the arch of the Covenant. He was grieved at the behaviors of Israel, and one day He gloriously left the temple and went back to Heaven (Ezek. 10).

Now, the LORD has returned as promised to redeem a people for His inheritance, to strike a decisive blow against Satan and the dark rulers; and He would do this through the death of His beloved Son.

When His hour had come, He prayed for His twelve disciples and for all of us who would later believe in Him, not that God would take us out of the world but to protect us from the evil one, and strengthen us by His Spirit so we wouldn't return to the bondage and slavery of the wicked one.

Jesus further prayed the perfect will of Jehovah-Elohim: That God would glorify Him with His own Presence, so that the Son would give glory to the Father; that the Son would in turn give Eternal Life to those of us who dwell in the valley of the shadow of death; and this Eternal Life would manifest the Name and eternal counsel of His will and purposes of God in us, and that the heart, Love and joy of the LORD would be realized in us too.

Notes

CHAPTER FIVE
WHO IS THE SON OF MAN?

"27 And beginning with Moses and all the prophets He explained to them the things concerning Himself in all the Scriptures. 11 For the Son of Man is come to save that which was lost" Lk. 24.27; Mat. 18.11(KJV).

Although Jesus of Nazareth was born in Bethlehem, Judea, the Christ in Him was from the beginning. Christ, the Word was with God as God. Jesus spent many hours with His disciples explaining that He is the incarnation in human form, the Creator of Heaven and Earth. He came unto His own people, the Jews and humanity as a whole, and they didn't recognize Him or believe that He was the owner of this vineyard.

This was mainly because Satan told them that he was the rightful owner and could distribute the land to whomever would be an obedient servant to him. What Satan said was not the whole truth: The Son of Man came to make war, to defeat and take creation away from him.

Yes, the Son of Man came down from Heaven to seek and to save what was stolen from Jehovah-Elohim in the Garden of Eden. Not only was God's family corrupted and shanghaied, but the earthbound Man lost his authority to rule.

In this are several substantial and compelling reasons why countless millions of truth-seekers past and present Christians, from generation to generation, all over the world believe that Jesus Christ, the Son of God, the Son of Man is the Savior of the human race. It is not only the fact that he made the claim, "I am the Son of God" (Jn. 10.36) that convinces everyone that He is who He says He is.

The people who lived during the terrestrial walk of Jesus were probably more skeptical that we are today. The Jews received the Word of God through Abraham the Hebrew who was born in Ur of Chaldea. He in turn taught it to his sons, and the Word of God found place in the hearts of humanity. So for centuries the Jews were familiar with the Word, scriptural promises and prophecies concerning the arrival of the Messiah, the Anointed One. And though there has arose many false prophets in the Old Testament and New Testament Church (even in the Body of Christ today) the true seekers of God were always able to recognize them.

We as creatures born in sin and conformed to the world have been implanted with iniquity---the desire to do what is wrong, even if we don't actually do it. We are prone to lying, manipulation, control and many have claimed that God or an angel appeared and commissioned them to do a work for them (many serial killers claim that God told them to punish "certain" sinners.) But in Israel these "messiah" impersonators or impostors relied on black magic, self-promotion and bribery to gain power and authority over their listeners.

But the statements of Jesus of Nazareth were not only backed up with Scripture that could be read and confirmed, but miracles, signs and wonders. Even after His death at Calvary, He continues to reach back from beyond the veil where He sits on the right hand of God, to perform even more miracles, signs and wonders through the Holy Spirit who indwells the true followers of Jesus Christ; and this is accomplished through a tangible, super-spiritual medium called Faith. No other religion, philosophy or their founders and leaders has ever accomplished this; neither has any of them raised from the dead.

The claims of Jesus Christ were backed up by His lifestyle. Although the majority of the Pharisees and Sadducees who made up the official Sanhedrin Council didn't agree, violently, and with murderous intent opposed Jesus' claim to be the Messiah, they didn't state, because they had no evidence, that He was a criminal wanted by the law or lived an immoral lifestyle; that He was lazy and wouldn't work, or that He was a beggar; that He was unlearned and ignorant of the Scriptures or even out of touch with Jewish traditions; but they did suspect that He was a prophet greater than John the Baptist, a scholar, teacher and the leader of a new sect.

Jesus has a unique character and lifestyle. He lives a holy lifestyle because He is holy; and so in the days of his humiliation as the Son of Man, He praised and worshipped the Father in Spirit and in Truth; He loved and honored His mother; His love for lost souls was and still is insatiable, in that He watches for and pursued after the lost; and rejoiced over His disciple's ministry successes, but grieved over those who refused to come to Him for rest.

He is a prayer warrior in that He is also the Priest of the Heavenly Sanctuary. He is meek, gentle, humble, compassionate concerning the sick whom He healed. He was intolerable of demons and the evil works perpetrated against humanity; He drove them out of people with His Sword, the Word of God.

With greater detail, God definitively pointed out the Messiah. He was altogether other than any man---past, present or future. The specifics of this Man is found in the Old Testament, a legal document written over a few thousand years; it contains more than 300 references to His coming. Using the science of probability and mathematics the chances of just 48 of these prophecies being fulfilled in one person is 1 followed by 157 zeros!

Therefore, the Old Testament Scriptures are 100% accurate, God-inspired and true. It is by faith and reasonable thinking that Jesus Christ is the Messiah and all the other titles that He laid claim to. He fulfilled the Old Testament prophecies concerning Himself, to the extent that He read to others about Himself. No one person could possibly fulfill all those prophecies---not even a hundred-man team of the best actors or magicians could successfully fulfill one of God's prophetic promises, that He has willed and spoken to come to past in the earth hundreds of years previously. These prophecies not only directly affected the citizens in the cities where they were given, but every nation to the end of the ages!

Here are a few of the testimonies concerning Jesus Christ:

Jn. 1.34 "I have seen and testify that this is the Son of God."--- John the Baptist 2.11 "…miraculous signs Jesus performed in Cana…" --- Apostle John 3.2 "…no one could perform the miraculous signs you do..." ---Nicodemus 9.16 "How can a sinner do such miraculous signs? --- Pharisees 11.47 "Here is this Man performing many miraculous."--- chief priests Lk. 4.34 "I know who you are--- the Holy One of God!"---unclean spirit 4.41 "You are the Son of God!"--- unclean spirit

Miracles, miracles and more miracles; these were not magic tricks or carefully orchestrated hoaxes. Human being who witnessed the miracles, signs, wonders, healings and deliverances testified to them. The Pharisees, priests, Romans---and even demonic spirits (who usually lie and it would have been to their advantage to say that Jesus was an impostor) shrieked in terror because Jesus is indeed God in a human (now glorified) body. And when an enemy says something positive about a person, it must be true. These miracles also prove that God the Father placed His seal of approval on the works of Jesus Christ; if Jesus was an Impostor, God would never in a billion years raise Him from the dead.

In Genesis 3.15, God said to Lucifer that He would raise up the Seed that would crush Lucifer's head: Consider it done.

Law of Empowerment

"Verily, verily, I say to you, He that believeth on Me, the works that I do, shall he do also, and greater works than these he do, because I go unto My Father"---Jn. 14.12 (KJV).

One thing that the Sanhedrin soon discovered about the followers of Jesus Christ is that His disciples were like Him. They noted that ordinary fishermen had been empowered with scriptural and godly wisdom far beyond their experience in the theological schools of thought. They also noted that the apostles had miraculous power like Jesus. No other person that they had known who claimed to be either the Messiah or prophet did the miracles that Jesus did or was capable of impartation---the ability to share their super-natural ability with others.

In the same way that the Prophet Elijah on his day of departure, left his prophetic mantle and ministry to the Prophet Elisha, Jesus left His authority and Anointing with His disciples. This perplexed---even vexed many of the Sanhedrin members, who knew that they had done a wicked thing in crucifying an innocent man, and now the Seed of God was multiplying astronomically, and the Sanhedrin was forced to reason that they had fought against God and lost.

Consistent with His leadership style, Jesus gave His Staff Members, the twelve disciples, His power and authority to represent Him everywhere He planned to visit. This delegated authority is known as the Law of Empowerment. It would not have furthered His eternal purpose in sending His disciples as ambassadors of His Kingdom amongst the people, if they weren't empowered to duplicate the success of their Leader; and neither would it serve the future plans of evangelism if the Church has no ability to manifest the plans, purposes, pursuits, likeness, authority and power of its Founder.

Not only did the disciples, the Twelve, but even the Seventy that Jesus pressed into service exercised spiritual authority to witness, to heal sicknesses, diseases and cast out demons; and they did this for the same reason: Love---to seek and save that which was lost. They did this with the same Agape Love, compassion and dedication as their Master, the Messiah, the Anointed One.

When the people saw the disciples manifesting divine unction, the miracles of Jesus Christ, they were convinced that these ordinary men had been reborn---somehow recreated and transformed into god-like. The people were immediately taught that anyone who repented of their sins and received Jesus Christ as their Lord and Savior, would be Saved and receive the Holy Spirit; and that it was the Holy Spirit, Christ within, who actually performed the miracles.

So we see that the leadership and management style of Jesus impacted the world around Him by means of delegation and ambassadorship, a mentoring and duplication process that has also become the standard of reference for leaders seeking political favor, networking, influence or increase in business market shares around the world.

Many of the spiritual principles work for whosoever will apply them, whether Christian or not; colleges and universities turn out students in cookie cutter fashion because the system they use involves spiritual principles that do not change with time, and are not subject to the stock markets.

Mentoring for Christ involves raising up spiritual sons and daughters to evangelize the city, state, nation and world; it should be top priority in the Body of Christ. But sadly most churches strive to lure as many Christians and non-Christians to their local congregations, then hold tightly onto us, work us like Hebrew slaves to further their finite vision (which might not be the will of God).

As earlier the subject of lying bishops and church leaders was mentioned, the behavior of many church leaders make the Law of Empowerment of none effect. Unlike Jesus, many of the churches are not interested in raising up spiritual sons and daughters; they are only interested is filling all the seats and preferably with people who have jobs! Ironically, the majority of sermons preached today---no matter what Scripture text is used---turns into a sermon about giving them more money.

When it's offering time, these churches have $500, $250, $100 lines (or other amounts). The Bishop or Pastor tells us that if we get in those lines---the lines with the "special" or colored envelopes, that we would get a better blessing than, perhaps, someone who only had $10 to give.

The Bishop stands watching, intimidating, his eagle eyes glaring, as we members of his congregation who are unknowingly under his witchcraft (manipulation, intimidation and domination) control, leap to our feet and run to those lines with our envelops held high so the Bishop can see and validate us as good, obedient persons; while our prideful spirit excels as we looks over at those seated who don't have the money or even a job like we do.

Some of these same churches require that we submit a copy of our W-2 Tax Form before they will consider us as members. This is for Tithing purposes. And if we don't give them the correct amount according to the W-2, we are no longer in good standing with that congregation. What a religious scam!

Later on in the week, after these churches have fleeced us of all our money, many of us are on the nationwide prayer lines asking for prayer because we don't have money to pay our mortgage, car note or utility bills. We can be seen by Christian, non-Christians, friends and relatives who know us at the food pantries and social services agencies because we have no food at home!

When our breakthrough comes, we "compulsively" run back to the same Bishop and church to testify what that ministry has done for us, and forget about the prayer warriors and intercessors who fasted and prayed for us. We often have promised to give an offering to help that little ministry grow; but for now, the spotlight is on us to keep on giving to the mega church!

The majority of these type ministries will not financially assist their members. They take our money but will not give any of it back; and if they are willing to help, they purposely embarrass and humiliate us, ask a lot of personal questions, check our tithing record, and if that is satisfactory, might give $100 towards a $1000+ debt, and tell us to go to Social Services, or some other organization where we haven't given our Tithes and Offerings, like we have faithfully done at that church for the last ten years. A lot of unnecessary debt and foreclosures could be avoided if we use common sense and not give money while under pressure from these money-hungry, controlling Bishops.

The majority of these ministries have incorporated such nonsense into their services that it has undermined the fabric and trust of the Body of Christ: To sell blessings at the highest bidder is an all time low for the Protestant Denomination. The old Roman Catholic Church with its Popes started this "Tribute, Indulgence and Extortion" iniquity. This type of behavior grieves the Holy Spirit, and He will have none of it!

Also the selfishness, insecurity, pride and egoism of many church leaders is terrible! Many are steeped in religious dogmas, traditions, false doctrines, greed and worldliness---some churches function more like the Mafia or other crime families than a place of security, nurturing and love; still others have too many high-titled, highly-paid officials overseeing too few people.

Many Church Leaders do not License or Ordain women, yet woman have proven their faithfulness, obedience, doctrinal accuracy and powerful anointing to Jesus and these Church Leaders. I (the Author) receive many requests from woman to join my Network of Churches and receive Ministerial Credentials.

These blessed and anointed Christian women truly love and respect their Church officials, but their Bishop or Pastor won't recognize their Calling; it is always the case that they gladly recognize and accept the women's tithes and offerings, or their services on the Deaconess Board (if allowed) choir, children's church, Usher Board or Nurse's Guild and other functions---but as a Licensed/Ordained minister preaching in their pulpit is a nightmare to them.

It is time to stop the control and ego-protecting! Mentoring spiritual sons and daughters is the Apostolic way, not heaping titles upon ourselves---such compound titles as Exalted Chief Apostle Bishop etc...

The Law of Empowerment allows for one person to raise up spiritual sons and daughters, who will in turn do the same. This allows us to spiritually duplicate ourselves thousands of times in our life-time. It will then be possible to evangelize the earth. Jesus sent the disciples ahead to evangelize the cities and towns before He personally got there.

In the **Battle for Life**, the enemy of our souls comes against those in Christian Authority more than any other persons that walks the earth. In order to effectively utilize the Law of Empowerment, we have to be set free from demons and our own flesh. If not set free from these things, we will wind up like the Pharisees who searched far and wide for a proselyte, then groomed them into the image of themselves, and make them more a child of Satan than themselves.

The fall of many church leaders is due to their doctrines and belief systems that are non-Christian in nature, which they pass on to their congregation, who in turn pass it on to their families, friends, social circles and business associates.

Inner Healing & Deliverance also deals with character flaws, those behind-closed-doors sins: Sexual perversions, homosexuality, fetishes, addictions and violence; those weird but strong cravings we often call the "freak" in us. If not dealt with, Satan will wait until we are leaders in the Body of Christ, then expose our "secret" to the entire world, causing many to stumble. This has happened to several well known and respected ministers. The results is that many people are hurt and fall away; some of them never return to the church.

Deliverance, Inner Healing or Emotional Healing includes being set free from certain people and their toxic personalities; free from their opinions of us, their expect-ations and control; free from being manipulated, intimidated or dominated by them; set free from being used and abused for their agendas, motives, sexual gratifications, satisfactions and ambitions; free from people living our life for us.

This is important because many church officials believe that we are sent to personally serve or idolize them; that we are, more or less, fans of theirs, to be used (even abused) by them, and then kicked to the curb when we are no longer useful, don't have any more money, or don't bow down to them. Many of the positions in these churches are based on seniority, tithing, cliques, popularity, personal appearance, wealth and family importance.

Some of these same ministers would have us believe that no one but them knows the Word of God; and dogmatically teach that no one else is Saved but those who belong to their ministry; plus, to top it off, tell us not to listen to other ministers, as though other ministers are not a part of the Body of Christ; neither should we visit other ministries, for fear we would be disobedient and defiled by demons or lose our Salvation. "Everything you need is in the house," they declare in a matter-of-fact tone. It is only manipulation.

Another thing to consider is that God will send people to us to warn us about our sinful behaviors: King David and Nathan the Prophet are a good example of God sending a prophet to rebuke a king; and if we will not repent and turn from our wicked ways, He exposes us, takes our ministry and gives it to another---as He took King Saul's throne and gave it to David, who was a man after His own heart---not a perfect man---but a human being with faults and frailties just like us.

At some point, many of us as Christian leaders stop depending on God to "supernaturally" provide our personal needs and the necessities of our local church. The enemy tells us that if we are going to be successful or outdo the congregation down the street, that we need to buy a multimillion dollar building. This will prove that we are more spiritual and have a solid relationship with God, and should shame that pastor down the street who has been laboring in his little church for twenty years, into thinking that something is wrong with him because we are so prosperous and blessed; it is the equating of material things with holiness and righteousness, when they are not even the same thing.

In believing that the (appearance of) prosperity means holiness, we begin tapping into the psychic and manipulative nature of the old man. Once there we come again in contact with the Law of Sin and Death, which is monitored and appropriated by the territorial spirits. We get that money for the building by instituting ungodly gimmicks, strategies, tricks, false doctrines, outright lies and deceptive practices; and anyone who doesn't like it can hit the street!

Thus many of us Church leaders are very powerful, influential and charismatic not because of the Holy Ghost, but because of the witchcraft that we use to get what we want from our congregation and from the political arena. Until one day the Lord pulls the cover off of us and we see our nakedness. We discover that we are less spiritual than a first year Christian.

REHEARSE, CURSE, REVERSE

1 "I do not ask that You take them out of the world, but that You will keep and protect them from the evil one. 17 Sanctify them (purify, consecrate, separate them for Yourself, make them holy) by the truth; Your Word is Truth. 19 And for their sake and on their behalf, I sanctify (dedicate, consecrate) Myself, that they may be sanctified (dedicated, consecrated, made holy) in the Truth"--- Jn. 17.15,17,19 (Amp. Bible).

When our life is not as the Word of God states that it should be we have to make quality decisions to do something about it. We can blame situations, circumstances, father, mother, husband, wife or even Satan---but in the end we have the choice to Rehearse it, Curse it, or Reverse it. God has a cleansing process that will wash away sins and reverse the stain that it left in our soul and mortal bodies. The cleansing process is called Sanctification.

Sanctification means to set apart for a special use or purpose, that is to make holy. The word sanctify comes from the Greek word "hagiasmos," meaning "holiness, consecration, or the process of sanctification." In this extended version of the word refers to the state or process of change, being set apart or made holy, to be partakers of God's holiness; in that God is completely "other" than human beings, we are brought into that state of "otherness" with Him.

Sanctification and holiness are relation-al: Only God is truly holy; everything else, whether it is people or things, are holy because of their relationship to God.

In the above Scripture, Jesus didn't ask the Father to take His disciples (or us) out of the world but to protect them from the evil one, meaning Satan and his demonic influence; which manifests as that dark influence working through the Law of Sin and Death, the world, and the flesh; it keeps us from accomplishing our assignments and being all that God has preordained us to be in Christ Jesus.

The Holy Spirit is in charge of the Sanctification process. We have an obligation to assist when led by Him to speak faith-filled words, behave a certain way and do certain things until they become natural to us. The goal of the Holy Spirit is to cleanse, purify and renew our minds. This is so we will have the mind of Christ. The process of Sanctification imparts the Fruit of the Spirit, instills Christian Character and moral change in us, the Believer.

The process begins at the moment the Holy Spirit arrives in our human spirit and Christian Conversion takes place. At the same instant Justification---being declared Not Guilty is decreed. Sanctification continues throughout our lifetime, as we are Saved and being Saved until Glorification Day---the Second Advent of Jesus Christ. The process of Sanctification can be rapid growth at times or slow growth; it depends on how low we have fallen, how much we resist the Holy Spirit, or how much we love the world and the things in it more than Jesus Christ.

Salvation and Justification are two sides of the same coin. Salvation comes through Repentance and Faith, and Justification is the legal standing of Salvation. Both address the issue of Adamic Sin, and what was accomplished at Calvary.

Sanctification also deals with the Law of Sin and death that feeds the inclination towards sinful behaviors that we all are born with; it also deals with cleansing, scares and effects of sins we committed before and during our relationship with God; for we did not suddenly stop sinning when the Holy Spirit resides within us.

Whereas, the work of the cross is past, present, and future, in that faith in the finished work of the cross is a spiritual weapon against the inclination to sin, and it keeps the Law of Sin and Death inactive.

Sanctification will be complete when the state of Glorification comes to all Believers. Glorification will transform our corruptible body into an incorruptible body; and death will be swallowed up in victory. This is also the era when the sons of God will be revealed and creation will cease to travail because the birth of the sons of God has become an eternal, even terrestrial happening.

As stated earlier, Jesus didn't pray that God would take His disciples out of the world without them first benefiting from the Day of Pentecost, when the Holy Spirit arrived to fill them and future Believers. Plus Jesus needed them to be witnesses for Him to build His Church.

This is the same reason that we are Saved and left on Earth for the process of Sanctification to change us to be more like Jesus; to display His personality, character, power and likeness, so that when people see our lifestyles they see a marked difference in us as Christians. Then they would be more willing to listen to our personal testimony and be willing to give their lives to Jesus.

3 "It is God's will that you should be sanctified; that you should avoid sexual immorality; 4 that each of you should learn to control your body, in a way that is holy and honorable. 22 "... the benefits you reap leads to holiness. 2.13 ... God chose you to be saved through the sanctifying work of the Spirit...1.2 "...chosen according to the foreknowledge of God the Father, through the sanctifying work of the Spirit, for obedience to Jesus Christ..."1 Thess. 4.3,4 Ro. 6.22 2 Thess. 2.13 1 Pet. 1.2.

In the Old Testament, Holiness applies to God, and its fundamental object lessons of types and shadows is that He is unapproachable; He is altogether other than anyone or anything alive. This un-approachableness is rooted in the fact that God is divine and set apart from His creatures and creation. Holiness in this sense is not merely an attribute, but something that is predictably found in God. He is holy in His grace as well as His righteousness, in His love as well as in His wrath; everything that He says or does is considered holy and above reproach.

"And one cried unto another, and said, Holy, holy, holy, is the LORD of host; the whole earth is full of His glory!" --- Isa. 6.3. Isaiah the prophet had an experience in the Presence of God. As a human being, he felt a sense of his own sinfulness, depravity, filthiness, issues, and inadequacy compared to God's perfection, majesty, worthiness, Agape Love and holiness.

Compared to the holiness of God, we feel in ourselves to be insignificant, negative in relation to positive, impure and sinful, and as such understandably an object of God's wrath. Who would want such a human filthy rag near them?

God revealed His Holiness in the Old Testament in various ways. He did it in terrible judgments upon the enemies of Israel (Ex. 15.11,12). He did it also by separating unto Himself a people, His inheritance, which He took out of the world to sanctify with a desire to make them partakers of His Holiness.

The Holiness of God is manifested in seven ways: His hatred of sin; His delight in righteousness; His never doing wickedness or sin; His separating the sinner from Himself; His punishment of the sinner; His great Love for the sinner; His redemption plan for the sinner.

The idea of Holiness is also applied to things and persons that are placed in a special relationship to God. The Holy Spirit, holy angels, Canaan Promised Land, city of Jerusalem, Arc of the Covenant, tabernacle and temple, Pentecost, Sabbaths and solemn feasts of Israel---they are called holy, since they are consecrated to God and are placed within the radiance of His Holiness.

The prophets, Levites, and the priests are called holy as persons that were set aside for special service of the Lord. Israel had its sacred places, its sacred seasons, its sacred rites, and its sacred persons.

However, the ethical idea of Holiness is different. We might be a sacred person, and yet live like a heathen, be entirely devoid of the grace of God in our heart; this ethical Holiness results from the renewing and sanctifying influence of the Holy Spirit. Holiness is expressed as relational. The idea of holiness is never that of moral goodness, in itself, but always the ethical goodness seen in relationship to God; not the works of the mind and flesh, or the keeping of any set of rules and regulations, but obedience to God's Word and His Spirit within us.

In the New Testament, there is a difference in the theology or application of Holiness. Holiness is seldom applied to God, though it is a reality, inferred, and quoted from Old Testament references. In the New Testament, the characteristics of the Holy Spirit, by whom Christians are sanctified, are qualified for service, and are led to their eternal destiny is the prime theme. The Greek word "hagios" is used in connection with the Holy Spirit of God nearly a hundred times.

The concept of Holiness and Sanctification, is ascribed to man as a process to change him into the image and character of Jesus Christ. Sanctification is never merely a moral improvement of the flesh, but a putting away by the Cross the deeds of the flesh---reckoned dead to sin and alive with Christ: Buried with Him in Baptism and raised with Him in Sanctification and Holiness.

Salvation, Sanctification and Holiness is not what the world or religious people think it is; it is not a New Year's resolution or turning another leaf, mental accent or engagement of the will. We would remain isolated, Sanctification and Holiness would be forever elusive and unobtainable by and through only the mind and its machinery. The Bible does not teach moral improvement or behavioral modification, but transformation and renewal of the mind via the agency of the Holy Spirit, after receiving the Salvation provided by God through Jesus Christ; it is primarily the Ministry of the Holy Spirit who sanctifies the Believer.

In the Word of God, Jesus insists on we being sanctified. Sanctification is that gracious and continuous operation of the Holy Spirit, by which God delivers the justified sinner from the corruption and pollution of sin, renews our whole nature into the image of the Son of God, and enables us to perform good works that are acceptable to the Father, as though they were Christ' s own works. In truth, these works are His because He wrought them by the Holy Spirit who dwells within us. The Holy Spirit empowers, motivates, and provides the eternal lifeline, connection and relationship with Jesus Christ and the Father.

Therefore, Sanctification is a work of which God and not man is the author. It differs from regeneration---the actual residing of the Holy Spirit in our human spirit--- in that we can, and is our duty to, strive for increasing Sanctification on a daily basis, by using every means that God has made available.

This is clearly taught in Scripture: "Since we have these promises, dear friends, let us purify ourselves from everything that contaminates body and spirit, perfecting holiness out of reverence for God" ---2 Cor. 7.1. In Colossians 3.5-14 is discussed the daily need to avoid sin.

So the **Battle for Life** remains a daily struggle against sin to obtain more Sanctification, which will help us to live holy (as differing from being declared holy by relationship with Christ); in the opposite sphere, it is a matter of submitting more of the self to God via the Holy Spirit: More of Christ, less of us, and we draw freely from the Law of the Spirit of Life that is in Christ Jesus.

Sanctification takes place in our heart but immediately affects what psychologist call the subconscious mind. After Salvation, which involves conversion and regeneration, the avoidance or curbing of sin must began. Our desire to sin has to be addressed. Therefore, the initial operation of the Holy Spirit is to focus and refocus our attention on the Word of God, praise, worship, faith, prayer and fasting to break the chain of our habitual thoughts associated and in relation to conformity to this fallen world.

WORSHIP

"A time will come, however, indeed it is already here, when the true (genuine) worshippers will worship the father in spirit and in truth (reality), for the Father is seeking just such people as these as His worshippers"---Jn. 4.23 (NIV).

The self-life that we possess is such that if we do not constantly monitor it, before we know it we would return to the old thoughts and behaviors. As stated earlier, a virus that has only been 99.9% destroyed can and usually does make a comeback and is more resistant to antibiotics than ever before; so it is with the mind of the flesh, the self-life; give the self-life an inch and it will take a mile; give Satan a ride and he will end up driving.

One act of faith is designed exclusively to take our mind off self and place it upon a Person who is greater than any human beingand that is to worship God. This act alone opens up the human spirit and soul to God, activates Faith and the Law of the Spirit of Life that abides in us; worship takes us into the secret place of the Most High where sits enthroned the LORD.

Also sitting with Him is the Church, in Him, which we are a part of. Through worship we are made conscious of our spiritual relationship, position and communion with Him; we come face-to-face with the lover of our soul, and are exceedingly glad with unspeakable joy and thanksgiving.

Many times physical and emotional healing come while we are in worship; this happens because we have forgotten about ourselves---surrendered that part of self long enough that the Holy Spirit can minister, make corrections and attitude adjustments, while bringing us into Kingdom alignment and order. Equally important is the fact that unclean spirits that may have entered into us through participating in sin, can be driven out during worship.

As the woman at the well came face-to-face with her sins by the loving Savior of the world, we too come face-to-face with our humanity, and are privy to things that only God knows. Because He loves and cares for us, He counsels us on these things, and guides us through our intuition, the ability of our human spirit to know something without having studied or experienced it---God helps us in the Battle of and for Life. He also tells us about things to come. We call this ability the Word of Wisdom and Prophecy.

Even from the days of King Solomon and the temple, the glory cloud only fell in response to the people worshipping. Jesus told the woman at the well that the hour has come where the true worshipper is not limited to being in a certain denomination or certain kind of building in a certain geographical area; but the true worshipper will worship God in spirit and in truth.

We don't worship God like the Pharisees or religious groups of the past, being unregenerate human beings, but as the New Creation in Christ Jesus, the redeemed, being the Children of the Resurrection. We worship and minister to the Lord Jesus Christ.

Jesus told the woman that she and the other Samaritans didn't know who they worshipped, because the Word of God came to the Jewish nation. It is the same today with the other religious beliefs, who pray and worship the God of their understanding, when the Word of God has come to Believers in Christ Jesus.

Worship, like prayer is a lifestyle and not something that we should do when we want something from God. In worship, God is well pleased because we have exalted Him above ourselves, family and famous people of the world. And in return, we become more Christ-like, because Jesus Christ, our High Priest is the worship example; in that like prayer, we worship the Father in the Name of Jesus. We worship God for who He is; we praise God for what He has done. Praise and worship go together as two sides of the same gold coin.

37 "When a woman who lived a sinful life…38 stood behind Him at His feet weeping, she began to wet His feet with her tears, then she wiped them with her hair, kissed them and poured perfume on them" Lk. 7.37,38 (NIV).

Jesus and His disciples were invited to dinner by Simon, a Pharisee. Very little is known about Simon, except that he belonged to the religious and political party know as the Pharisees, who were one of the two Jewish factions which made up the Sanhedrin Council. Whether Simon was a follower of Jesus, curious, or was on assignment from the high priest to get evidence against Jesus is not known. One thing for certain, he was in the right place at the right time for a lesson on worship.

The woman came prepared to worship her Lord. She brought an alabaster box of perfume; it was expensive, which showed that she was a woman who would spare no expense to worship the Lord. She was also a prostitute with a desire to be set free from her sinful, excessive compulsive behavior. She humbled herself and washed His feet with her tears and dried them with her hair; then she anointed His feet with the perfume. She never spoke a word but her actions spoke louder than any words: Worship.

Simon saw her and was disgusted. He didn't realize that she was a new breed of worshipper. What he saw was a prostitute who had intruded into his home, uninvited, and was interrupting his religious experience; she was an emotional drama queen. Simon didn't realize how her sinful lifestyle had driven her to despair, to the breaking point; sin, like a rusty chain, had dug into her flesh and infected her entire soul, and she wanted to be free from it. Simon spoke in his heart but Jesus knew it as though Simon had said it aloud, "This Man, if He were a prophet, would have known who and what manner of woman this is that touches Him; for she is a sinner" (Lk. 7.39).

Simon obviously didn't regard himself as a sinner. He thought that since he was a member of the Pharisees, and an educated Jew, that he was better than the common people. A spirit of pride in his accomplishments wouldn't allow him to believe that he was no better spiritually than a murderer, thief, drunkard or prostitute; and that his righteousness was as filthy, smelly rags in God's sight.

But Jesus loved Simon anyway, for the way that Simon thought was typical for those blinded and lost in the natural realm of demonic corruption. Jesus told him a parable about a certain creditor who had two debtors; one owed 500 pence and the other 50 pence. Both were forgiven the debts. Jesus asked Simon who would love the creditor the most? Simon, being intelligent, answered correctly.

Then Jesus turned to the woman and showed Simon his thinking distortions: Jesus told Simon that when Simon's family, friends, priests or Sanhedrin Council members came to his house, he furnished water to wash the dust off their sandaled feet, and kissed them on the cheek, and supplied oil to anoint themselves; but Simon did none of these things for Jesus or His disciples.

Yet the prostitute washed Jesus feet with her repentant tears, kissed and dried His feet with her hair; this kiss (Gr. Proskuneo) was more like a faithful dog licking the hand; then she anointed His feet with expensive ointment. "For she loved much, but for whom little is forgiven, the same loves little" (Lk. 7.47).

True Worshippers are givers---we are not just people with our hands up in the air because someone told us to do it or everyone else is doing it; we would be pretenders. Neither is it possible for a selfish, stingy person to be a true worshipper, because we are too busy trying to hold onto what we have; our fist are closed so tight that our hands are not open to give or receive from God. God said in Exodus 23.15 "No one is to appear before Me empty-handed."

True worshippers are broken people. The alabaster jar must be broken before the entire contents of worship is released as sweet-smelling perfume in the nostrils of God. When our outer hard shell of the self is broken, the results is the release of the human spirit to worship Jehovah-Elohim, the Creator. Worship is a way to "come out from among them" and be with God; to forget about ourselves and concentrate on Him, to worship Him.

Corporate, private worship, praise and prayer are four ways to destroy the works of Satan in our lives. The act of worship diminishes our self ambition, the self-life, by causing us to decrease in importance; these four limit the desire to continue in present sinfulness. Because of the Healing and Deliverance power in worship, is the reason that Satan comes against us; praise teams and prayer warriors experience the same resistance. This is because we put pressure on the territorial spirits rulers, and make them work harder. At times during worship weeping takes place. Men find it difficult to weep. Men are told that it is "unmanly," and so the enemy steals our worship. David was a true worshipper. He danced with all his might before the Lord and didn't care what people thought. Worshippers cannot go unnoticed; and because of peer pressure, many of us refrain from exuberant worship because of what others think, for fear of being talked about, ridiculed or even passed over for promotion.

Michal, King Saul's daughter who was given in marriage to King David, criticized him for dancing down the street as he celebrated the Lord's victories in battle. She was a hater because her brothers who were next in line for kingship were passed over by the Lord in favor of a man after God's own heart. And though she was married to David, she despised him in her heart.

Michal was spiritually barren and wanted David to be barren also. But David continued to praise the Lord anyway; he told her that she hadn't seen anything yet, and danced even harder! (2 Sam. 6.10). The outworking or her sinful comments was that she went childless the remainder of her life.

8 "Again, the devil took Him to a very high mountain and showed Him all the kingdoms of the world and their splendor. 9 All this will I give you," he said, "if you will bow down and worship me" ---Mat. 4.8,9 (NIV).

Jesus told the woman at the well that God seeks true worshippers; but Satan also seeks worshippers too! When we are Born Again and make God the object of our worship, Satan tries to corrupt it. Satan knows the power of worship to set the captives free and comes against it every chance he gets; therefore, fear of man becomes a snare, a major obstacle why we Christians do not worship with our whole heart:

"What will people think!" We say to ourselves, or rather, the spirits impress on our reasoning that we are weird, strange, embarrassing ourselves and unspiritual. Because worship is personal and a function of the heart, and should not be canned or strictly regulated, the religious cliques dismiss it as unnecessary. They say, "It don't take all that! Why don't she go someplace else with that crying and falling out on the floor every Sunday morning?!" Worship remains controversial; there are so many variations and styles; but worship remains the avenue to the heart of God, though it has resulted in many church splits.

Simon the Pharisee represented the religious class in his day. He was all traditions, laws, rules and regulations; his spirit was not free. Simon also represents what God doesn't want: Worship-less, dead local churches. Dead churches full of dead people with only Bible theological knowledge, human relationships called family and friends, but not the Anointing to destroy the yoke, the Spirit of Worship; but the woman at Simon's house represents today's worshipping local churches.

In Rev. 4.9-11, in Heaven, the Elders fall down and worship before the Throne of God. They are examples of how church leaders should also be worshipers. Titles and positions don't make us a worshipper. But in fact, a Pastor who is not a worshipper usually stays in his office until it is time for the offering! These leaders, and there are many, with their negative attitudes and nonparticipation stifle the worship that others desire to offer God.

Ro. 8.1 states "There is no condemnation for those who are in Christ Jesus." God, through the Holy Spirit, doesn't condemn us but convicts us of our sinful actions and lifestyle. This conviction leads to repentance; but condemnation leads to despair. God isn't interested in condemning us but in redeeming us.

Conviction of sin motivates and gravitates us towards God, but condemnation leaves us estranged and powerless. The act of worship reaffirms this scripture by removing the stain of sin once forgiven through repentance and faith; we can approach the Father without feelings of guilt, because our sins are washed away; guilt gets in the way of true worship; we cannot worship God if our attention is on what we did wrong the day or hour prior to worship.

Worship increases our faith; our increased faith destroys the yoke of sickness and brings wholeness including prosperity. Sin is forgiven, curses broken, devils driven out, love, joy and peace reside Spiritual pride was Satan's downfall. Pride robs up from experiencing the wonders of worship. All out worship starves the ego, whereas pride restrains our voice, our tears, and keeps out hands below our waist. It takes great determination to lift our hands high to the Lord and sing praises and worship to His Name without caring what people say.

Being set free from demons is a good feeling within itself! But there are some of us who, like the plantation slaves, don't want to be free from those spirits whom we walk in agreement with. And in the end, will not benefit from worship, but will likely be barren, our nakedness exposed to the nature and influence of the demonic community, until such a time as our sin is publicly exposed or we are taken home, that is, providing we were actually Born Again to begin with.

"And when all the children of Israel saw how the fire came down, and the glory of the LORD upon the house, they bowed themselves with their faces to the ground upon the pavement, and worshipped, and praised the LORD, saying, For He is good, for His mercy endures forever"---2 Chr. 7.3 (KJV).

Although this is an Old Testament scripture, God does not change. King Solomon prayed and dedicated the temple to God; we pray and dedicate the human temple to God. Fire came down from Heaven and consumed the burnt offering; we are that offering, a living sacrifice, presented to God as our reasonable service. The fire of the Holy Spirit is resident in our human spirit.

The fire, the Holy Spirit comes down and out of us at the same time. The Holy Spirit consumes the guilt and uncleanness, and drives out sicknesses, diseases, addictions, phobias, perversions and anything else that we do not need in us---those weights that so easily beset us and slow us down from being all that we are called to be in Christ. The journey through this Physical Realm is long and hard; there are many temptations, distractions, detours, dead ends, demons and human deceivers. But tis so sweet to trust in Jesus!

CHAPTER SIX
CHRISTIAN FREEDOM

18 "For in the first place, when you assemble as a congregation, I hear that there are cliques (divisions and factions) among you...21 For in eating{Communion} each one {hurries} to get his own supper first (not waiting for the poor) and one goes hungry while another gets drunk" 1 Cor. 11.18, 21 (Amp. Bible).

The Battle For Life also involves the Wars of the Lord. These are successive battles fought by the Lord in order to reestablish His Word and Name; the reestablishing of His Word, because Adam failed to honor and obey it, and thus the creation was subject to deterioration and corruption. His Name, His reputation was not honored by Adam, and thus Lucifer became the god of the Physical Realm of time, space and of corporal existence.

After Satan incited the Jews to murder Jesus of Nazareth, he thought that this single stroke would cripple God's plan to retake the world from him; and at the least, he thought that God would be forced to raise up another Savior of mankind to return to the vineyard, and he, Satan, would be waiting to kill Him too. But Satan didn't count on the death of Jesus to be the strategy and Wisdom of God; that God would utilize even the wicked actions of the devil and his friends to redeemed His Inheritance.

However, since Satan failed to impede God's plan of Salvation, he will do all that he can to keep this New Creation from being all that God wants us to be. The religious Jews, the Sanhedrin Council, persecuted the church with jealousy, envy and legalistic vengeance.

Saul of Tarsus, now the Apostle Paul, was an extraordinary example of the grace of God, unmerited favor toward a man who persecuted the church, but was now a leader. For this, the Jews hated him even more. Saul had once worked for them in their zeal to rid the earth of Christians. Paul had the authority and arrest warrant to bring Christians back to Jerusalem to stand trial for heresy.

Arrested Christians had no chance of a fair trial, many of which were beaten or stoned to death before they arrived at Jerusalem; and those who did make it were destined to be thrown into a den of lions or other wild beast. But the Word of God flourished in spite of the devil and his interference.

Now Paul was instructing the Corinthian church on how to be true Christians. He explained to them that the Christian faith was not an extension, not something added to the Judaism faith, but entirely new; they had to give up the old religion for a spiritual relationship with Jesus Christ.

Being In Christ meant the old traditions, legalism, circumcision and worship was obsolete; the new creature was altogether other. And though the church was in its infancy, there were abundant Spiritual Gifts. There were so many manifestations of Spiritual Gifts that the spirit of pride infiltrated in and incited the Christians to argue amongst themselves which apostle or Spiritual Gifts were more important, and whom amongst them was the most anointed.

Not only were the Jews pressing the Christians to keep the Law, traditions and ceremonies, but demonic spirits of lust, fornication, lying, perversion, greed, frivolous lawsuits, defiling the Communion Service (the Body and Blood of Jesus) and other behaviors threatened to corrupt, make them morally and spiritually unfit to fellowship with God, who is Holy, and thus invoking His Justice instead of His Grace and Mercy (1 Cor. 5-14). This was the devil's attempt to provoke

God to punish His own people, after the Blood of His Son was shed at Calvary.

1 "O foolish Galatians, who hath bewitched you, that ye should not obey the truth... 2 Received ye the Spirit by the works of the Law, or by the hearing of faith? 3 Are you so foolish? Having begun in the Spirit are ye now made perfect in the flesh?" ---Gal. 3.1-3(KJV)

The Apostle Paul had a similar conversation with the Galatians church. The spirit of legalism had almost persuaded them to go back to Judaism. Their liberty in Christ Jesus was threatened. Galatians who were saved by Grace through Faith attempted to be made perfect or complete through the keeping of the Law of Moses, a Law that was not Faith-based but was added because of transgressions. Paul used the word "bewitched" because he knew that it was black magic, the manipulation of their minds; it was the same spirit that hounded the Israelites to return to Egypt and continue in slavery.

Today, many Christians say that they want the church to be like the early church. But the early church was an infant; when we were infants we could not walk on our own or even feed ourselves; we had to be nurtured, breast or bottle fed, protected, taught right from wrong, and this was accomplished by adults.

The early church struggled with immorality, like today; they had abundant and powerful Spiritual Gifts, like we do today, yet the early church was often led by carnal leaders, ruled by the flesh, and by the influence of the wicked principalities, whose goal was and still remains to defile the Bride of Christ.

Even today many Christians believe that we need to add to Christianity either another religion, something that amounts to a different philosophy or cult. For example: Martial arts is great for self-defense but the philosophy that accompanies it is Buddhism; we sometimes quote those sayings of Buddha, a Hindu, or some equivalent Chinese sayings, as though they are equal to the Word of God; the same applies to fortune cookies, astrological charts or the zodiac.

Thousands of Christians are also Eastern Star Masons, and this is a cult; still other Christians who were formally members of Islam or another religion retain and honor the former traditions, mannerisms, fellowships, attend ceremonies, read the books, collect their art work and other detestable objects that may attract legalistic, religious demons from the Adamic Curse of the Law. Detestable objects---material objects that are psychically connected to activity that God deems as detestable---gives evil spirits the legal right to harass, corrupt and authority to drag us away from the protection of Christ.

Thousands of Christians read both the Holy Bible and the Koran, and actually believe that both are equal in importance---equal in being holy and God-breathed; that the Koran explains or supplements the Holy Bible, that Mohammad was sent from God to finish the work of Jesus Christ!

It has also been said by many Christians---including pastors---that all men are brothers; this genealogical truth is only according to the unregenerate flesh without the Holy Spirit and not the New Creature in Christ Jesus.

THE PROTESTANT MOVEMENT

During the persecutions of Christians by the Sanhedrin in Jerusalem, the Christians dispersed into other countries and lands. As they went, they spread the Gospel of the Kingdom. Then, when the Roman Empire persecuted them also, they fled even deeper into the known world. And though it was actually the territorial spirits that incited the authorities to ban Christianity and destroy its followers, it furthered the plan of God to reach the entire world with the Message of Grace through Jesus Christ, the Light and Life of the world.

And so the dispersed Christians sought a place where they would have freedom to worship the Lord Jesus without the officials of established religious organizations and governmental agencies controlling them.

Then after the home goings of the Apostles of the Lamb, Apostle Paul and the early church officials, the official church---what was visible to the naked eye—slowly took on the design of men; it declined into an organized religious bureaucracy whose purpose was to manipulate, intimidate and dominate the lives of the human population; it turned into another tool of the devil to enslave the souls of mankind. But, of course, this was not the real Church; because of persecution, the real Church went underground to survive the demonic assault.

A considerable amount of the New Testament Faith-based doctrines and teachings of Jesus Christ were lost, or rather, intentionally omitted; these omissions were primarily due to the church leadership non-acceptance of Biblical Doctrines, and refusal to be led by the Holy Spirit.

The leadership, full of spiritual pride, intended to continue a lifestyle of corruption and blatant sin, lust for wealth, political power, and they caused millions to stumble and fall away from the true faith in Jesus Christ the Lord.

In a swift, calculated move, the rounding up of Christians under one human leader was implemented by the territorial spirits; but this was only the official church; the real church couldn't be eliminated by these entities. This human being was called the Pope; he was granted the highest leadership honor, authority and god-like obedience; he was stated to be God's only representative on earth; his headquarters was

Rome, Italy, the home of the Roman Catholic Church. The Pope was deemed infallible according to the doctrine of "absolute infallibility of the Pope".

Pope Innocent 111 (1198-1216) wrote: "We may according to the fullness of our power, dispose of the law and disperse above the law. Those whom the Pope of Rome doth separate, it is not a man that separates them but God. For the Pope holdeth place on earth, not simply of a man but of the true God." And Pope Nicholas 1 (858-867) declared, "the appellation of God has been confirmed by Constantine on the Pope, who being God, cannot be judged by man."

Spiritual pride and self-righteousness was only the tip of the proverbial iceberg of what the Catholic Church---operating in parallel with the true Believers had declined towards: Manipulation, intimidation, domination, fear, bribery, extortion, tortures, imprisonments and murders soon became the usual instruments of religious activity working towards world domination.

Vast armies marched off to war against countries who wouldn't pay Tribute to the Pope and Rome; they were fought because that country would not fill the treasury chests of the Bishops sent to collect the money. Several wars were fought against the Moslems who would not fill the Bishop's treasury chests, or kneel and kiss their rings, nor would they deny their faith and become a Catholic.

Another practice that led to the degradation of humanity was the outrageous practices of the Roman Catholic Church of selling Certificates of Indulgence: This was the receiving by donation of large sums of money by the church so that a person would not be punished by God or authorities for past, present or future sins---be they premeditated or not! Such a policy especially benefited wealthy sexual sinners who found pardon for their murders, fornication, adultery, homosexuality and pedophilia.

Another practice and policy that brought a considerable income to the Roman Catholic Church, that for a considerable fee, the dead relatives stuck in Purgatory (stated as a holding place for the dead) for sins committed in life, would be released to Heaven simply by making the agreed upon payment---this was also the case for children who were said to be stuck in "Limbo" and couldn't get to Heaven. By greasing the holy palms of the Bishops. As soon as the coins hit the bottom of the treasury chest, the deceased was said to "fly away" to Heaven.

REFORMATION

When Jesus ascended to Heaven and assumed His rightful place at the right hand of the Father, He send back to earth the promise of the Father: The Holy Spirit (Acts 2.-5). The mission and work of the Holy Spirit is to glorify Jesus, indwell the Believer, seal and position us in the Royal Family, lead, guide and conform our thinking, purpose and spirituality to that of the Lord Jesus Christ.

The Holy Spirit, the true Reformer, began to bring reformation to the Church. St. Jerome (1370-1416) was born in Prague, Germany. He created the Latin Vulgate as a translation for the common people. Up to this point, copies of the Holy Bible were scarce, and only the Catholic Church officials had copies; and the copies were written in Latin; therefore, the people only had the word of these officials what was in the Word of God; plus many of the commoners couldn't read anyway.

Now, with St. Jerome's translation, the people were not solely depended on the Roman Catholic Church. Of course, the Catholic Church didn't like what Jerome had done, and he suffered dearly at their religious hands. It took some of the authority, power and control over the masses out of their hands.

Jerome was arrested and imprisoned for over a year. He went before the Council of Constance, and without the benefit of a lawyer or self defense, was found guilty of heresy and condemned to burn at the stake as a heretic. Jerome was chained to a stake. Dry grass and wood was stacked under and around him. The material was lit. As the fire raged he was heard singing a song about Jesus.

In the 14th Century, John Wycliff (1377-1384), a native of Yorkshire, England, and theologian arose to throw off the papal yoke of tyranny with his Bible translation to take the place of the dying Latin Language. Not only did he dare to translate the Word of God on his own, without papal permission, but he made dozens of copies of his illegal manuscript. Wycliff's radical actions threatened the spiritual and political power and control of the Catholic Church. He introduced the possibility that laypersons could now read and interpret the scriptures for themselves. The Roman Catholic Church taught that one had to be a priest or higher to understand the Word of God; that one had to be blessed and commissioned by the Pope to receive such lofty understanding and revelations. Wycliff's thinking bypassed the indoctrinations of Catholicism.

As expected, the territorial spirits and official church officials struck back at him---hunted him down like the U.S. hunted Osama Bin Laden---and tried to discredit Wycliff's divine revelations, even to the point of threatening his life.

After years of debates, banishments and persecutions by the Catholic Church, John Wycliff died in his sleep at age 56. He was buried; but 31 years after his death, still angry with him, the Council of Constance removed his remains from their burial place, burned them, and threw his ashes in the river. Haters!

The wind of the Holy Spirit blew in the life of Dr. Martin Luther (1483-1546). He was born in Eisleben, Saxony. The Catholic Church, calling itself the one true church, was now in position to receive a great reformation. Since the average Christian had access to the Word of God without the Catholics, the original New Testament Doctrines could be revived. Martin Luther, and others, challenged Rome. The new Christian sect were called Protestants because they protested the doctrines and authority of the Roman Catholic Church.

Dramatically, Martin Luther nailed what became known as his 95 Theses on the door of the church. The Holy Spirit used him to declare certain truths from the Word of God that had been purposely hidden from mankind.

A partial list of the reformation truths revealed in his 95 Theses:

Christians are justified by Faith; Saved by Grace through Faith, and not of human efforts or decrees, but by the shed blood of the Atonement of Jesus Christ.

Repentance and Faith is necessary for Conversion, producing outward signs of a change of heart through a change of behavior. Christians are to lead a life of Repentance; Godly sorrow works repentance. The act of confessing to the priest without true repentance in the heart is meaningless. True Repentance had not been practiced by the Church if Faith is to be real, alive and affective.

The Pope has neither the will nor the power to remit guilt or penalties, unless the penalties are his own to issue or remit. The Pope is not God---but a mortal man, subject to sin, mistakes in judgment, sickness, disease and death like the rest of humanity. At the most, the Pope is a servant of God.

He is not by far the only instrument or servant of God on the earth.

The canonical penalties apply only to those who are still alive, none are binding to the dead (as applied to people believed to be in Purgatory.). Death puts an end to all the claims of the earth-bound Church canon; like the living spouse is no longer bound by marriage to the deceased spouse, and vice versa.

The practice of selling Indulgences is unscriptural. A dead person cannot be absolved, forgiven of sins, or saved from every canon penalty by the Pope or any of his agents, nor other human beings. Money cannot buy Salvation, Faith, Grace, Repentance, Forgiveness, Divine Healing, or Heaven; however, Hell can be obtained by the misuse of money to advance evil in the heart or in the world.

The true treasure of the Church is the Gospel of Jesus Christ.

If the Pope could liberate people from Purgatory, why doesn't he do it out of love---a most holy attribute---and compassion for the lost, instead of money?

It is unscriptural to pray for the dead, no matter where they are.

Mary or the deceased saints have no authority to pray for the living. Christians should not pray to Mary or try to communicate with the deceased.

Christians should be encouraged to follow Christ through the Holy Spirit.

Obviously, when the Pope read the 95 Theses (95 propositions) he sent Bishops to dissuade the former Augustinian Hermit, and if that failed to demand his appearance before the Council. Rome did all that was in its power to arrest Martin Luther, but he had Spirit-led officials and friends who believed that he was right, and that the Roman Catholic Church was wrong and should be dissolved.

From his safe places, for years Martin Luther preached the true doctrines of the Bible to everyone who had an ear to hear. His critics aggressively attacked him verbally, by letter and book in a vain attempt to discredit him. As much as they would have been thrilled to get their hands on him, Martin Luther died of an internal sickness. Before he died he recited his favorite Scripture" For God so loved the world, that He gave his only begotten Son, that whosoever believeth in Him should not perish, but have everlasting life" (Jn. 3.16). Then he closed his eyes, left his mortal temple and went to Heaven.

THE NEW WORLD

The enemy of our souls has not developed any new strategies. In the same diabolical fashion that Satan enticed Eve in the Garden, his intent and out-workings remain the same. Using people outside of our Christian faith is one strategy, using those within our faith circle is another; then there are family, friends, coworkers and bosses that he can use to make our lives harder than it already is; or use our own selfish and domineering self-life is still another way in which the enemy gets control of us and limits our freedom in the Christian Faith.

Try as he did, Satan was not able to keep us from personal contact with God through the death of His Son Jesus Christ. But now that we are Born Again, Satan attempts to limit our freedom, love, joy and peace that comes with spiritual growth---by any means necessary---and turn our joy into sorrow, our trials and tribulations into misery---so that we leave this world with curse words on our lips instead of praise and worship to God.

Nevertheless, in all our afflictions, He too is afflicted. He never promised that we wouldn't have trials and tribulations, but does promise to be with us through them all! It rains on the righteous and the unrighteous alike, and the sun shines on the just and unjust.

Christian freedom involves the right to worship the Lord Jesus Christ without fear and persecution. Persecution, as with Jesus Christ and his followers, often comes from those who belong to other religions and sometimes from non-religious or political groups, who are jealous, envious, or hating because of the joy, praise, worship, prosperity and singing that we do.

The masses of people are miserable and looking for someone to blame or strike out at. Often, we as Christians wind up being that group; not to mention the fact that Satan hates us above all creatures who ever walked the earth; he hates us more than the Jews; he hates us because we have Christ in us; he hates us because we have authority over him; he hates us because we have eternal life and he lost his---that is, one day he will be destroyed and cease to exist.

But, for the most part, non-religious groups don't care about religious matters as long as we don't adversely affect their financial situations; the main reason that they interfere in Church matters is that the territorial spirits have control of their minds and uses them to do their evil deeds.

Still another reason is that the unsaved are terrified and don't want their children to hear about Jesus and be converted towards righteousness; God's Presence would be in their homes and within their children, who would quote Bible verses in the home and make the parents uncomfortable, because the demons in and associated with them would be unsettled and agitated.

But there are also many secular businesses whose livelihood comes from the supplying of religious organizations and cults with those items they need to practice their beliefs; and they have hardened their hearts so, that being around Christians doesn't affect them at all.

Religious persecution is why the early church fled Jerusalem and later had to flee Rome. After that, when the Roman Catholic Church emerged as a dominate authority, persecution took on a whole new meaning: The Crusades, the persecution of Moslems, Jews and Protestants.

Again, the enemy turned on the earthbound Church to destroy it from within: The persecution of Protestants against Protest-ants! The divide and conquer strategy was being used. The Baptists against the Lutherans, the Lutherans against the Methodist and Catholics----all claim to be followers of Jesus Christ and the one true Church, but the difference in doctrines and interpretations from the same Holy Bible brought them, with the interference of the demonic hierarchy, to blows and murder in the name of what was actually religious self-righteousness without a true relationship with Jesus Christ.

The moving from one continent or place to another to escape religious persecution only gives temporary relief but doesn't solve the problem. We cannot run from Satan; he has to be resisted after we have submitted our entire being to God; then and only then will he flee from us.

Therefore, we cannot go anyplace where he is not because he is the god of this world. The only place that we can go where he isn't present is in Heaven. If it were possible for us to travel by spacecraft a million light years from earth, we would still be in his domain, and the evil tendencies, iniquity, sickness, disease, death and the Law of Sin and Death would still be active, effective and working in and around us.

In the 16th Century, several of the British North American colonies that eventually formed the Unites States of America were settled by the Pilgrims, who fled the European religious tyranny and persecution. The New England colonies: New Jersey, Pennsylvania and Maryland were established by people who sought after freedom to worship God in a manner they thought was right and proper. They purposed have a fresh start in the new world.

But the secular settlers, many of them criminals and fugitives released from the prisons providing that they left the country, came with them to the new world to get rich and continue their lawless life-styles; who in the end hoped to take over the colonies and make them non-religious like themselves.

In other words, they journeyed to the new world in search of "freedom from religion" in Europe instead of "freedom of religion "to worship the Lord Jesus Christ. So now there are religious people and secular people together in the new colony, both bringing their mental baggage and beliefs into a new territory.

The first winter almost wiped them out; many of them died of the freezing cold and starvation. The local Indians: Algonquians, Iroquois and Susquehannok Indians pitied them, brought them food, blankets and helped them to survive the winter. That summer the Indians taught the colonist how and what to plant in the soil. They were few and the Indians were numerous, so they made a treaty with the Indians to always be at peace with them, and to help if another Indian nations attacked or went to war with them, and vice versa.

Eventually, as more ships arrived with people, they attempted to indoctrinate the Indians and make them Christians. They bought more land from them because the colonies were growing. They slowly pushed the Indians inland.

Then a few genius settlers decided to take the land from the Indians without paying them. And so the Indians retaliated and went to war with the "Christian" colonist, who in turned killed the majority of the Indians and continued expanding their Christian settlements.

The convictions held by both Catholics and Protestants (Protestants includes Puritans, Lutherans, Baptist, Methodists) of the religious colonists was their belief was the one true faith, and that it was the duty of the civil authorities to impose it---by force if necessary---to the end of saving souls from Hell. Those who didn't believe or adhere to their philosophy could expect no mercy and were subject to persecution, imprisonment or execution as heretics.

The atrocities included torture, starvation, imprisonment, hanging, drowning, mutilations and burning at the stake. Hence, the real Church was still underground, so those caught speaking in other tongues meant being burned at the stake as a witch or warlock; any supernatural manifestations of Spiritual Gifts was construed as demonic and worthy of death if not repented of; ironically, those things that were done in Europe to them, they now were doing to themselves and others in the new world colonies.

The majority religious groups controlled the political offices and punished dissenters. Therefore, in some areas the Catholics controlled and persecuted the Protestants; and in turn, in Protestant territories, they persecuted the Catholics; and in other areas the Catholics and Protestants persecuted the non-Christian settlers, including the Indians, whom they vigorously sought to convert from heathenism to Christianity, but had very little success.

The Indians viewed Christianity as some-thing to add to their own religious beliefs; for the most part, they didn't believe but acknowledged it to please the colonists. The Indians were truer to what they believed in than the colonist were; they were not quick to convict their tribesmen, and their punishments fit the crimes committed; and even when the death penalty was imposed, it was humane and without prejudice---and had nothing to do with religion.

The Puritans were English Protestants who desired to purify the Church of England from what they deemed to be undue influence of the Roman Catholic Church. In 1630 the leaders of the Church of England grew intolerant of them, so an estimated 20,000 Puritans emigrated to America in search of liberty to praise and worship God as they chose. They met with the Puritans who arrived in December of 1620, who suffered many causalities and were almost wiped out in their first winter, where they almost froze and starved to death.

Unlike the Pilgrims who came to Massachusetts in 1620, the Puritans believed that the Church of England was a true church, though it needed to be reformed. They thought that once their experiment settlement in America was successful, the Church of England would follow their example. They were sadly mistaken.

However, the Holy Spirit is the only one who can bring reform. When a denomination is as far gone and removed from righteousness as the Church of England or the Roman Catholic Church was, it takes generations to weed out and dissolve political-religious corruption from a denomination than is demon possessed, flesh-oriented, secular, and little more than a criminal organization of spiritual fugitives hiding from God in His own church building!

The New England colonies were called "Bible Common-wealths" because they claimed to seek the guidance of the

Holy Bible and its authoritative Scriptures. Scripture was cited as authority for many criminal statutes.

It is true that they had the Bible verses at their disposal, but the intent of their hearts were as callus and legalistic as the Pharisees were in Jesus' day. The colonists were legalistic, judicial, without love and mercy; they usually sought the most severe of punishments imaginable; their perverse and sadistic demon-like henchmen were diabolical and too unnerving to be called Christians; they enjoyed their duties too much, and seemed to receive pleasure from the pain and misery of others.

The leaders of the colonies believed that their zeal would please God and turn the hearts of people to Him through repentance and faith; when it is godly sorrow that lovingly brings about repentance---not being stretches until the joints are separated and bones broken on the rack!

In fact these Christians were only destroying people's lives instead of saving them; they did the work of Satan disguised as religious devotion; whom God required mercy instead of sacrifice; He required repentance and faith of the heart instead of forced confessions screamed out under duress of wretched pain from torture, or the feared flames of raging fire at the burning stakes of iniquity.

Later the Massachusetts Constitution of 1780 declared that: "the happiness of a people, and the good order and preservation of civil government, essentially depend on piety, religion and morality." They agreed that the Word of God was the source of enlightenment, the scriptures provided the way to Life---they called it religion---that is unparalleled in its ability to unite and sustain the family unit which makes up the state and nation.

Faith in God is more powerful and cohesive than faith in a constitution, self and in man. Principles have to be practiced not talked about. Although the principles are in the Holy Bible, we are not holy by reading the principles, but by practicing the principles. The Word without the Spirit makes the Christian hard and legalistic. Then we are more apt to seek the punishment of a transgressor than forgiving them and seeking their best welfare and soul salvation.

"...kings shall be nursing fathers, and their queens thy nursing mothers"--- Isa. 49.23.

Before 1776, the churches received financial support from their state benefactors, called "nursing fathers" (Isa. 49.23) and the citizens paid a "religious tax" to support the church and church-run public schools. But because the Christian denomination that was in political power in a particular state and region received the majority or all of the tax money, brought dissent, a push by the Baptists and theological liberals for a separation of church and state.

The Baptists, who had grown strong since the "Great Awakening" felt that it was inherited wrong to permit a single denomination to monopolize state support, and that the churches should not be supported by the state taxation anyway, but by individual free-will tithes and offerings; and this movement was not spearheaded, as one would suppose, by the non-Christians, but the Christian Baptists themselves.

As sometime enemies will unite for a common cause, the Catholics didn't want their children going to Protestant schools anyway, whereas, Rome supported the Catholic Churches in America, and, whenever convenient, extended their long arm across the ocean to influence the destiny of America.

The religious-political struggles continued for decades. The Christians fought and jogged for position amongst themselves, to gain total religious-political control of the colonies. There was some divine Light and Truth revealed;

but there was significantly more religious, legalistic and schemes leaning towards bondage, darkness, corruption and manipulation from the territorial spirits.

The enemy worked through the non-Christians too, and waited in anticipation for the outcome, a possible single Christian winner to emerge. Later, they would confront and challenge the Christians to separate them in other ways when it was time to frame the U. S. Constitution, Articles and Amendments.

The future plan was to elect and seat a Congress of non-Christians that were susceptible to cohesion, bribery and immorality, and steal the country away from Jesus Christ; once sufficient seats in Congress and the Supreme Court were won, the country would revert back to the influence and iniquity of the territorial spirits whom the Pilgrims and others previously fled for their lives from Europe.

A convention met in Philadelphia in 1787 and adopted the Constitution of the United States. Article VI, which stated that "no religious Test shall ever be required as Qualification" for federal office. This opened a huge door for non-Christians to not only hold political and judicial offices but to lead the so-called Christian nation (Yet, the President of the United States must be native born).

In 1791, the First Amendment in the Bill of Rights forbade Congress to make any law "respecting an establishment of religion, or prohibiting the free exercise thereof." So, other than these references, the U.S. Constitution was framed with very little mention of Christianity, which was the main reason that the Christians came to the new world.

In the guise of protecting the Christian Faith and its principles, the general inclusive wording also opened up the newly formed United States to legally be bound to accept other religions: Islam, Buddhism, Hinduism, Judaism and other religions, cults and philosophies plus their prac-titioners---including atheists, witches and black magic warlocks to be elected into government offices---since there was no Religious Test to pass.

The United States became a melting pot of diverse trad-itions and cultures not unlike Europe, Asia and Africa; but with a Constitution guaranteeing everyone the right to worship their gods on equal ground as Christians who were the grassroots founders of the United States, who risked their lives and buried their love ones during that first harsh winter.

Many of the religionist complained that the U.S. Constitution, or rather its framers, slighted God by opening up the nation to every wind of doctrine. But the answer they received was that the Constitution was framed by committed federalists, who believed that the power to legislate religion---if there were such a place---lay elsewhere, perhaps the individual states, not the Federal Government.

Plus the framers stated that if they wrote into the document too much "denominational" or Christian language that the different factions in Christianity and non-Christianity wouldn't agree with the wording, no matter how delicate and precise it was written; and it would not be ratified by the various states that formed the Union. They insisted that the document was not totally "irreligious", but was designed to bring together a union of states under one government and flag, at a time when everyone was at each other's throat!

MELTING POT

"Give me your tired, your poor, Your huddled masses yearning to breathe free, The wretched refuse of your teeming shore. Send these, the homeless, tempest-tossed to me, I lift my lamp beside the golden door!"---Emma Lazarus: the Statue of Liberty. The Statue of Liberty is located on Liberty Island, a 12-acre plat. The Statue was a gift of friendship from the people of France to the people of the United States and is a universal symbol of freedom and democracy. The Statue of Liberty was dedicated on October 28, 1886, designated as a National Monument in 1924.

When asked, most people consider the Statue of Liberty as an image that symbolizes America's immigrant heritage. She has watched over New York Harbor since 1886. On her base is a tablet inscribed with words penned by Emma Lazarus in 1883. Now far away is Ellis Island, where thousands of immigrants entered the United States.

France is in Europe, and this is one of the countries who persecuted the Christians and forced them to leave because they found them undesirable and unwelcomed. Now, as a symbolic reference, the French declared that America has become a melting pot---an iron pot with scrap metals thrown into the same pot---of people and religions like Europe was in the past and is today.

It is to imply that the Pilgrims and Puritans who exodus from Europe in the 1600s in the pursuit of religious freedom was a waste of time, if a century or so later they wound up in the same situation: A melting pot of non-Christian people having control of the government, courts, schools and businesses.

The Battle for Life is such that we cannot, other than through physical death, remove ourselves from the battle. As long as we are living in a corporal body, we are in for a fight to the finish; and since this is truth, we might as well give the enemy such a headache that he goes and harass someone else who is more willing to cooperate or listen to his mess!

The Christians from Europe were persecuted by the territorial spirits using human beings as their physical hands; to escape the human instruments only brought temporary relief; this relief was short lived until the evil spirits found someone else to use, and in many cases it was fellow Christians in and outside of the respective denominations.

As we have discovered, Satan is a master at dividing groups of people against themselves. He brought division between the colonists and the Indians; the treaties were broken and both factions killed innocent women and children. The colonists went on raids and wiped out entire Indian villages: Women and children were not spared; the Indians retaliated and butchered entire families. The majority of this activity was incited by the territorial spirits; and this kind of activity, including subtle forms of it, goes on all over the world even today.

Since the U.S. Constitution was framed, people from all over the world have come to America in search of religious and social freedoms guaranteed under the protection of the Constitution. Basically, everyone who is in this country--- legally or illegally---should be protected by the Constitution as far as their life is concerned. But the full benefits should be reserved for those who are citizens.

We have the Supreme Court of the United States whose Justices have the duty of interpreting the intent of the framers. Because times, customs and what is termed "morality" "normal" or "acceptable" non-criminal behaviors shifts from time to time, the Justices are supposed to adhere to the literal intent of the Constitution, and not the whims of the military, politicians or citizens. It's interesting how the military can initiate operations all over the world, and Congress votes to wage war against other nations without voter approval, then on top of that, legislates moral issues by passing laws contrary to the doctrines of the Church.

However, through political pressure, weal-thy corporation lobbyist, special interest groups like the ACLU (American Civil Liberties Union), Gay and Lesbian rights, abortion rights, immigration, death penalty, MADD, and others---the Justices have increasingly handed down decisions in favor of these groups, based on their "modern" liberal interpretations of the Constitution.

These decisions ultimately strike down Christianity as the only true faith and make it equal to all other religions; and the scriptural Word of God, ordinances and moral codes of ethics are not to be considered absolute truth, infallible, but optional and outdated for this modern fast-moving in-the-know society.

To the Justices, It is acceptable behavior for citizens to lead a Gay or Lesbian lifestyle, therefore they cannot be discrim- inated against in marriage, employment, tax deductions, and can adopt children if they wish, who in turn will likely teach these children that it is alright have this "alternative" lifestyle.

Atheists, witches or other non-Christian persons can enjoy the protection of the Constitution: "Life, liberty and the pursuit of happiness" any way that they can find it. And when they are elected to office (Many Christians vote for persons we know are not good moral examples) they use their positions to help elect others just like them, and thus they gain more political strength to guide the state, nation and world in the direction where the territorial spirits demand.

America has become a land opened to the world and its influence. It has become a place where the Bible and prayer has been taken out of the schools and replaced by metal detectors, drugs and armed gangs. Spiritually---where it really matters---constitutional freedom not to become a Christian is not necessary, because we are not made a Christian through an act of Congress anyway! But exer- cising this right or freedom from Christianity is more dangerous than its benefits, especially when there are several religious beliefs to choose from, meaning several kinds of hidden land mines around us and our children, that the enemy of our souls can activate and destroy our soul, ruin our eternal life and have us shipwrecked on the shores of Hell. Freedom of religion (in its positive meaning) and freedom from religion are not the same.

Yet, there is always the fanatical exception that can be argued that because we in America have Freedom of Religion, there are no Blasphemy Laws such as are found in Pakistan and other Arab Countries. These laws make it a crime punishable by death for a male who speak out against Islam, the national religion; women may receive life in prison. There, Christians are arrested, imprisoned, beaten, burned alive in the public streets and executed. So, in this context, America seems like heaven compared to the Middle East.

Notes

CHAPTER SEVEN
APOSTLES & PROPHETS

"Surely the Sovereign LORD does nothing without revealing His plan to His servants the prophets"--- Amos 3.7 (NIV).

The Battle of and For Life began in Genesis. In Chapter Six the record of the calling and commissioning of Noah was found. Noah was the first of God's prophets. God called him to deliver His prophetic Word to a people who enjoyed riotous, wicked living, a people who refused to walk by faith, but instead walked by human impulses, emotions, human knowledge and eye sight.

Noah obeyed God and built an ark, which is also a symbol of the ark of safety that is found in the loving and protective arms of the Messiah. Being in the ark is being In Him, and having no righteousness of our own but having an imputed righteous that is by Faith in Jesus Christ.

Noah's ark was like the boat that the Twelve Apostles rode in when the storm came. Jesus was also in the boat. The Lord got up from His rest, and rebuked the storms that were in the lives of those in His ark of safety.

God, who because of the lawlessness of mankind, in His divine Judgment and indictment, extended His mercy towards mankind for 150 years by allowing Noah to preach and prophesize the coming destruction of the entire world; yet God would not lift a finger to execute His will until He first revealed His plan to his servant, the Prophet Noah.

In Genesis Chapter Twelve, the story of Abraham began. In it Abraham was called of God. He left his kindred, to go to a place that God later show him. God revealed His eternal plan to Abraham, that Abraham was (already in His eyes) the father of many nations, and that the entire world benefited from the Promise and Blessing; this Promise and Blessing was the Seed, Jesus Christ; the Messiah, the Holy One of Israel who crushed the serpent's head.

Abraham believed and trusted in the words of God and his faith was counted to him as righteousness. Not only did Abraham become a friend of God, but he also became a prophet of God.

"And the LORD said {to the destroying angels}, Shall I hide from Abraham that thing which I do; seeing that Abraham shall surely become a great and mighty nation, and all the nations of the earth shall be blessed by him?" (Gen. 18.17,18). Here again is an example of how God elects to work through and with those who are His prophets (and New Testament Apostles) before He will do anything substantial, anything that would affect the course of a nation, society, human history and experience (especially His New Testament Church).

Throughout the Old Testament, whenever civilization declined to the point that the righteous Judgment of God conflicted with His Mercy, God raised up deliverers like Moses; Judges like Samuel, Samson, Deborah and others. He also sent prophets to the people to intercede---from Noah too John the Baptist---to persuade Israel, the children of God, to repent and turn from their wicked, flesh and idol-worshipping ways.

God first sent the Word to the king of Israel. The king was responsible for the spiritual, moral, economical and social welfare of his subjects. But more often than not, the kings "did evil in the sight of the Lord," and refused to listen to the men of God. When the king could have been a good example of godly Light to the people, they chose to remain in total darkness. By doing so, they consented to slavery rather than defending Israel from slavery; they led the people who admired and trusted them further into darkness than perhaps they would have went on their own. (The same is the situation today with our political leaders).

God raised up and called good and faithful men like Isaiah, Jeremiah, Ezekiel, Daniel and others into the vineyard to preach the Word and intercede---stand in the gap between Him and the people. But again the Children of Israel, the unborn Church, refused to abide by the Word of God. But in direct response raise up their own false prophets and teachers to tell them what they wanted to hear, and not what they needed to hear from the Lord. They loved the darkness more and rather than the Light of God's truth. They enjoyed the revelations of the sensual flesh, the whispering in their itching ears, and pseudo visions during their sleep---the fellowship of the territorial demons; they loved it more and rather than the sweet Holy Spirit of Love. And so, they murdered the Truth-bearing prophets, and preferred religious slavery over the abundant Life. Therefore, the Old Testament closed with a 600 year silence, until the birth of John the Baptist who prepared the way for the Lord Jesus Christ.

THE NEW TESTAMENT CHURCH

19 "The household of God...; 20 And are built upon the foundation of the apostles and prophets, Jesus Christ, Himself, being the Chief Corner Stone"--- Eph. 2.19,20 (KJV).

Jesus Christ, our Lord and Savior is no different towards His Apostles and Prophets. Even in the days of his humiliation, He discussed with His Apostles the details of His mission, death, burial, resurrection and Exaltation. He also told them that as His Father works, He works; because He and the Father are One.

Jesus told Peter that upon the revelation that Peter had, that Jesus is the Christ, that He would build His Church, and the gates of Hell will not prevail against it; and even though the Earthbound Church may stumble off the path into one ditch or the other, the powers, influences or strategies of the territorial spirits will not quench the Light of Christ, or drive the Light from His Church; because the Church is built upon a unique foundation: The Apostles and Prophets, with Jesus Christ being the cornerstone, the stone that determines the direction and square of the building, and is inscribed with the date it was laid.

The Twelve Apostles of the Lamb were those who walked with Jesus during His earthly journey. After Jesus ascended, He send back the Holy Spirit to indwell Believers (Acts 2), and multiplied blessings of Ministry Gifts :

"It was He who gave some to be apostles, some to be prophets, some to be evangelists, and some to be pastors and teachers. 12 To prepare God's people for works of service, so that the body of Christ may be built up,13 until we all reach unity in the faith and in the knowledge of the Son of God and become mature, attaining to the whole measure of the fullness of Christ" Eph. 4.11-13 (NIV).

Satan pulled out the stops to put an end to the ministry of Jesus Christ. He thought it was a master stroke to kill Him, so he could carry on business as usual. He worked feverishly manipulating the Jews and Roman authorities to accomplish his goal: To murder the Prince of Peace. Of course, he was not wise and discerning to know that it was the plan of God all along to sacrifice His Son.

When Jesus ascended on High, He sent the (Five-Fold) Ministry Gifts designated to continuously, throughout the ages, buildup and strengthen the Church, the Body of Christ. As stated early, two of the Ministry Gifts are part of the foundation of the Church: The Apostles and Prophets.

The Apostle is a New Testament counterpart to the Judge of the Old Testament (like Samuel), and the New Testament Prophet is not sent to Israel alone, but has a broader function---even to the nations of the world.

Again the enemy stretched forth his hand to vex the church: He has convinced many denominations that the Church doesn't need a complete foundation---that it doesn't need Apostles or Prophets in order to function until Jesus returns; that the Apostles and Prophets were only necessary to start the church with doctrines, signs, wonders and miracles, but all that is past!

Most Christian denominations accept the ministries of the evangelist, pastor and teacher, but refuse to recognize and accept the Apostles and Prophets as being necessary and a vital part of the whole, the Church. But they dare not say they don't need the third part of the foundation---the Chief Cornerstone, Jesus Christ, for fear that they would be labeled non-Christian.

If our car had a six cylinder engine and it was only running on four cylinders, we would experience a severe lack of horse-power; it wouldn't run efficiently at all; and if it was missing two spark plugs, thus leaving to open holes in the engine where they belong, it wouldn't start at all.

This is the situation in most churches: A lack of anointing, a lack of miracles, signs and wonders; a lack of power over the flesh because of the lack of Ministry Gifts; the Apostles and Prophets are also given to function in the local churches.

Where the two vacancies are, the enemy has two open doors to come and go as he wills; Satan will also pull members of our congregation out through those empty places, and out of the protection of the church, where the Apostles and Prophet are supposed to be posted.

The evangelist, pastor and teacher are readily accepted worldwide. But the offices of Apostle and Prophet are slowly being defined and accepted in the Charismatic, Pentecostal and Nondenominational churches.

The "ascension gifts" are scripturally given; they are needed for the Church to fulfill its destiny here on earth. "For the perfecting of the saints" was the kind intent of the Lord Jesus Christ in giving the gifts. If the Church did not need them, He wouldn't have given them.

We miss out on the fullness of the measure of Christ, the yoke-destroying power of a well-oiled (anointed)and maintenance church, without the presence and impute of the Apostles and Prophets; two ministries that are directly anchored to the Lord Jesus Christ, the Chief Cornerstone.

To refuse something or someone whom Jesus Christ has given to help us is not unlike the children of Israel who refused the Prophets and even killed them. We may not physically kill an Apostle or Prophet, but we refuse to listen to them and even assassinate their character by running our mouth against them, by spitting venom with our acid words of contempt and spiritual pride; our own ignorance being fueled by the same spirits who persecuted the Prophets in the Old and New Testament; then we wonder why we have so many issues, health problems, barren and are not growing spiritually or even materially!

Jesus is called the Chief Apostle (Heb. 3.1). He is also called Prophet (Mat. 21.11), Shepherd (Gr. Pastor), and Teacher (Jn. 3.2). He also is The Evangelist (Jn. 4.4). Having in Himself the Five-Fold Ministry Gifts, He delivers to the Body an expression of Himself spread out over the entire

Body, but uniquely concentrated (as are the Spiritual Gifts that accompanies these offices) in these five offices.

If we, like in our natural employment, had an office that is given to us by our employer; and this office has all the equipment, computer and technology including an inexhaustible reference library to do the job, we would get more work done there than in our automobile or walking down the street. So it is with the Ministry Gift offices that are empowered with Spiritual Gifts and direct access to the Employer. We as Apostles and Prophets can accomplish more for Christ.

"In reading this, then, you will be able to understand my insight into the mystery of Christ, which was not made known to men in other generations as it has now been revealed by the Spirit of God's holy apostles and prophets"---Eph. 3.4,5 (KJV).

Apostle Paul, who wrote two-thirds of the New Testament, stated that the mystery of Christ has now been revealed through the Apostles and Prophets; he did not say through the evangelist, pastor or teacher---but through the Apostles and Prophets. It stands to reason that the Apostles and Prophets receive a greater degree of revelation knowledge than the other gifts, through the other gifts are important in their duties to make up the fullness of the Body.

Paul wrote this several decades after Jesus had resurrected and ascended; he was not talking about the Old Testament Prophets, though they did receive abundant revelation of Christ, but the New Testament Apostles and Prophets, in whom the mystery of Christ was revealed.

Apostles and Prophets are to continue throughout the Church Age, until "we all reach unity in the faith and in the knowledge of the Son of God and become mature, attaining to the whole measure of the fullness of Christ" (Eph 4.13).

"Husbands, love you wives, just as Christ loved the Church and gave Himself up for Her to make her holy, cleansing Her by the washing with water through the Word, and to present Her to Himself as a radiant Church, without stain or wrinkle or any blemish, but holy and blameless"---Eph. 6.25-27.

THE CHURCH NEEDS APOSTLES & PROPHETS:

Has all the Church members reached unity? No. Has all Church members acquired the knowledge of the Son of God? No. Has all Church members matured? No. Has all Church members achieved the whole measure of Christ? No. Are all Church members without stain, wrinkle or blemish? No. Has the sons of God been revealed? No. Has Jesus come back for His Church? No.

The Earthbound Church is not complete, therefore the sons of God are not yet revealed (Ro. 8.19-23). The Five-Fold Ministry are to operate in the Body of Christ on earth until the second Advent of Jesus Christ. At which time the sons of God will be revealed; mortality will be changed to immortality, and then the Five-Fold Ministry Gifts will not be needed because we will be complete. "to wit, the redemption of our bodies" (Rom. 8.23)---made perfect through Glorification, which is the completion of the Holy Spirit's process of Sanctification.

The word "apostle(s) occurs 85 times in the New Testament but is not mentioned in the Old Testament, meaning that the Apostle is a gift of the Dispensation of Grace; it is an office and person approved and appointed by Jesus Christ as is evident in the four Gospels of the appointment of the Twelve Apostles, and later Luke writes of Matthias replacing Judas Iscariot as an Apostle (Acts 1.15), Paul, Barnabas (Acts 13.1) and others were sent out as Apostles.

It really doesn't make a lot of sense why the majority of Christians do not believe that there are or should be Apostles and Prophets in the modern Church. This is the results of exclusion by the local church pastors; it is religious persecution, prejudice, fear, ignorance, control and the insecurity of local pastors who are convinced---deceived by the church-dividing spirits---that the Apostles and Prophets would come into their church to tell them what to do, or steal some of their tithing members (many pastors don't care about non-tithing members leaving), or expose the religious nonsense that is being taught.

The offices of Apostle and Prophet are different, though one compliments the other; both the Apostle and Prophet have Spiritual Gifts and receive divine revelations. Because of this, the local pastors shun and even discourage us from communicating with these gifted saints, and often discourage these Ministry Gifts from being a part of the local congregational church.

The pastors fear that the Apostle and Prophet would undermine their authority and challenge their decisions; so they often teach us that there are no Apostles or Prophets in the modern church, and if they claim to be such—and we listen to them, we are disobedient and some type of God-sent punishment would befall us; it is as though they try to curse us.

Many pastors are very insecure about their position in the Body of Christ, and use manipulation and other psychological maneuvers to maintain control over the thoughts and actions of those of us they believe personally belong to them. Pastors refuse to allow these men and women access to their pulpits to teach or preach the full gospel, in hope that they would get discouraged and leave the local church (or even the entire city).

Sometimes the pastor may purposely humiliate, anger make light of the Apostle or Prophet to create a hostile environment in order to find something to hold against them for the purpose of discrediting their ministry and personal credibility before the congregation or board members. Then they stick out their chest and say, "I told you that he wasn't an Apostle. Did you hear what he said to me?!" Apostles and Prophets are not perfect, and the devil's attacks are more frequently.

CHARACTERISTICS & MINISTRIES

"Enter ye in at the straight gate: for wide is the gate, and broad is the way, that leads to destruction, and many there be which go in there: 14 Because strait is the gate, and narrow is the way, which leads unto Life, and few there be that find it"--- Mat. 7.13,14 (KJV).

The Apostle is called of God and not by men; a true Apostle is not called by proclaiming himself or herself an Apostle, but by revelation and confirmation by Jesus Christ, and through the agency of the Holy Spirit, since the Holy Spirit speaks on earth and in the Church in behalf of Jesus Christ.

Neither does a pastor, evangelist or teacher have the authority to make anyone an Apostle, when they are not themselves an Apostle: Apostles beget Apostles, as pertaining to the ceremonial setting apart the Apostle: The Holy Spirit shares the Chief Apostle title with Jesus Christ, the two being one Spirit.

The characteristics and ministry of the Apostle (root means "sent") is always in relation to the foundation of Christianity.

Even in the Old Testament era, when Israel was overtaken by their enemies or strayed away from the path to worship false gods and doctrines, Jehovah-Elohim raised up Judges to lead them out of the physical and demonic bondages.

Even so, are the Apostles sent forth to set the congregation, the Church free from the bondages of false doctrines that have infiltrated into the Earthbound Church. When the local churches have lost the True Way, grope and feel around in the darkness---a darkness and blindness demonically imposed---the Lord raises up Apostles to lead the church, out of the right or left hand ditch, back onto the Narrow Road. God also raises up Prophets to prophesize to us words of warning, faith and encouragement to those who are in religious captivity.

In **The Battle For Life**: The above Bible Scripture doesn't only apply to those who are lost and without Salvation, but to those of us who are Saved but find ourselves off of the Narrow Way and treading the muddy bottom of a religious ditch, dug for us by none other than the territorial demons and those human being who are their willing and unwilling servants.

Of course, no one individual other than Jesus Christ has all the following characteristics without measure. The below list is also a composite of characteristics found in the New Testament Prophet. The measure or degree of anointing and gifts depends on God's plan and purpose for our life.

Acts 2.4 Apostles are **filled with the Holy Spirit.** Acts 2.14-36 Apostles **preach the Word of God.** Acts 3.1-8 Apostle **Heal the Sick**. Acts 4.1-12 Apostles are **persecuted.** Acts 5.1-11 Apostles pronounce God's **judgment.** Acts 5.12 Apostles work **signs and wonders.** Acts 8.14-17 Apostles **lay hands** on others to be filled with the Spirit. Acts 8 Apostle are founders of **new churches and ministries.** Acts

10 Apostles are sent to preach in **other nations.** Acts 14.23 Apostles **ordain pastors and elders.** Acts 15.1-21 Apostles settle **doctrinal disputations.** Acts 16.18 Apostles cast out **demons.** Acts 19.22 Apostles **Send forth other Apostles to** minister. 1 Cor. 3.10 Apostles are master builders who lay **spiritual foundations.** 1 Cor. 4.14-15 Apostles give **warnings** of pending judgments. 1 Cor. 7.1 Apostles counsel pastors and answer biblical questions. 1 Cor. 11.34 Apostles set **churches in Kingdom Order.** 2 Cor. Apostles **edify the Body of Christ.** Eph. 2.20 Apostles are part of the **foundation** of the Church. Eph. 3.3-5 Apostles prophesize and receive **revelation** directly from God.

FROM CALLING TO COMMISSION

"For many are called but few chosen"---Mt. 22.14.

The purpose of this study of Apostles and Prophets is to reveal the relationship between the absence of the two offices of Apostle and Prophet to the decrease of authority and power in the local churches, a decrease in the ability of pastors to live the supernatural and moral Christian lifestyle before God and the world; and the effect that it has on the evangelists who brings the people to the pastors to be nurtured in what is supposed to be a safe, loving and spiritual environment, but often turns into a religious, controlling, manipulative, deviant and sexual pit that does more harm to the young Christian than good.

The absence of the Apostles and Prophets from the foundation opens the door for demonic activity. Such a tremendous absence ties the hands of the Prayer Warriors and Intercessors, from pushing back the forces of darkness that come against the local churches. The huge hole left in the protective shield surrounding the church, is an open door to every seductive and hateful spirit to twist the minds of pastors until they are exposed as weak "sinners" before the finger-pointing world, and those Christian haters we discussed earlier.

Those who love the darkness more and rather than the Light of Christ would proclaim, "That's why I don't go to church---the pastor is a hypocrite! He is an alcoholic who sleeps with prostitutes!" In the natural realm, the information they have is the truth, but not the whole story on that pastor's life. If the haters could walk in his shoes for a year they may have fallen even further than he did. Apostles and Prophets provide more power to the Body of Christ to walk in Authority, Holiness, Righteousness, Truth and Deliverance.

Another problem that is facing the Body of Christ is a sudden appearance of false prophets and false apostles. Whenever there is the real thing, whether in the secular business world or the Christian Church, we will discover that the counterfeiters want their piece of the action. In the case of the local churches, the territorial spirits create such confusion that we don't know who to listen too---who is the real or false apostle or prophet? We will know them by their fruit!

The Calling and Commissioning of the true Apostle or Prophet in the Christian Faith is not based on self-promotion, church board hierarchy promotion, human worthiness or persistence in prayer, petitioning God to bestow the honor and assignment; and there are no modern day Apostles or Prophets of God outside of New Testament Christianity.

The prophetic ministry of John the Baptist was the last of the Old Testament genuine Prophets of God. Prior to the Exaltation of the Lord Jesus Christ, the arrival of the Holy Spirit to seal and indwell Believers, and the unique New Testament Covenant mantle placed upon the Apostle and Prophet, the remaining Judea prophets either converted to

Christianity, or eventually died under the Old Testament Covenant.

Jesus said in John 15.16, "Ye have not chosen Me, but I have chosen you, and ordained you." This is based on God's Sovereignty, Election, Predestination and Calling, in that He chose---before the foundation of the world---Apostles and Prophets (and other members of His human family) to serve Him in this capacity, to be special ambassadors for Christ,

"Though He were a Son, yet learned He obedience by the things that He suffered. And being made perfect, He became the author of eternal salvation unto all them that obey Him"--- Heb. 5.8,9.

To whom much is given, much is required; therefore, the Apostle has to undergo and learn discipline: Obedience, faith, prayer life, morals, integrity and biblical doctrines. As the Word states that Jesus learned obedience by the things that He suffered, and was made perfect though His obedience, the Apostles and Prophets are made complete and competent by a wide range of life experiences, in which wisdom is gained through spiritual, intellectual, emotional, and often traumatic experiences; that all things may work together for the good, to create empathy for the struggles of the lost and downtrodden, the beaten-down ones who have lost their way; to create keen perceptions of what is needed in the stand against the ruling spirits; to convert humanity to Jesus Christ, and buildup the Body of Christ for His return.

The Apostles and Prophets are required to hear from God more accurately than the other members of the Body of Christ, to reveal God's specific Word, will, plans, purposes and pursuits.

We should not take it lightly to call ourselves Apostles or Prophets just because we have the gift of prophecy (which is a Spiritual Gift not the Office of Prophet), organizational skills or are good at administrative functions; there's more to these offices than that. but Christlikeness.

The Apostle Paul states the correct attitude, the centrality of Christ in the thinking of the Apostle and Prophet: "But whatever was to my profit I now consider loss for the sake of Christ. What is more, I consider everything a loss compared to the surpassing greatness of knowing Christ Jesus my Lord, for whose sake I have lost all things. I consider them rubbish, that I may gain Christ and be found in Him, not having a righteousness of my own that comes from the Law, but that which is through faith in Christ. I want to know Christ and the power of his resurrection and the fellowship of sharing in His suffering. "(Phil. 3.7-10).

There is more to being an Apostle or Prophet than someone telling us in a prophetic conference that we are, reading books on the subject, or even going to theological school and graduating with a Doctorate Degree. Bible college is a great way to obtain biblical knowledge; but biblical knowledge and the Calling of God are not the same thing, though God may send us to school as preparatory.

Paul writes of forgetting about our own accomplishments or failures---be they past or present---and embrace the attitude of pursuing and obtaining Christ, the High Calling of God, and count everything else as rubbish (King James Version says dung), and put an end to self-promotions, self-glory, self-will and self-preservation; to suffer loss of the love of the world and all that is in it, for everything that God has called us to; and press purposely and upward for the mark of the prize of the High Calling in Christ Jesus.

Many are called, but few chosen (Mat. 22.14). Like the Special Forces Units of the United States Army, many solders try out for this elite group, but few actually complete the rigorous training to become America's Best.

Even so, many Christians receive the high calling and ignore it; others receive it and don't want to go through the preparation; still others, having become religious, worldly and self-centered, have the wrong attitude, and therefore never press pass the Calling stage to the Commissioning stage.

And yet there are even some Christians who are Called but have not been released as Apostles or Prophets, but have gone out on their own----and therefore are not "sent" ones but "went" ones. Being unprepared, these Christians do more harm than good because people see their obvious rough edges, lack of discipline, lack of integrity, scanty bible knowledge and no anointing; hence, no miraculous, signs and wonders accompanying their ministry. Plus, by their inexperience and bad behavior, they prejudice the local churches from listening to the Commissioned and seasoned Apostles and Prophets.

There can be a lengthy time between the Calling and Commissioning. Bible examples of God's process for taking us from Calling to Commissioning varies.

Abraham was called at age 50; after 50 years Abraham progressed from Calling to Commission. Joseph waited 13 years before he saw a partial fulfillment; then he had 80 years of successful leadership and ministry. David waited 17 years for a partial fulfillment of the prophecy; then he had 40 years as king of Israel. Elisha waited 12 years as an apprentice of Elijah; then he had 50 years of prophetic ministry. John the Baptist waited 30 years for his Commission, and it lasted about 2 years before he was executed; Jesus said, born of woman, that John the Baptist was the greatest of prophets. Jesus of Nazareth waited 30 years for His Commission, and it lasted about 3 ½ years before He was crucified; now He has an eternal ministry as Head of the Church, King of Kings and Lord of Lords. The Twelve Apostles went through 3 ½ years of training. Judas

Iscariot wasn't Commissioned because he betrayed Jesus and then hung himself. Apostle Paul waited 17 years; his ministry lasted over 30 years.

God's preparation process applies to all who are Called; but to be Chosen is to finish the course and keep the faith until released and Commissioned. We cannot be like Judas Iscariot, who betrayed Jesus for 30 pieces of silver, later to find his neck in a noose and hanging from a tree; we cannot allow our Calling to be cut short through greed or love for the things of the world; we kill the Calling by being impatient, rebellious or lifted up in pride.

ACCOUNTABLE TO THE CALL

29 "For the gifts and calling of God are without repentance {irrevocable}." 19 God is not a man, that He should lie; neither the Son of Man, that He should repent: hath He said, and shall He not do it? Or hath He spoken, and shall He not make it good? 20 Behold, I have received commandment to bless: and He hath blessed: and I cannot reverse it"--- Ro. 11.29; Nu. 23.19,20.

The Apostle Paul stated very passionately of how he pressed towards the mark for the prize of the High Calling of God. With this press comes a tremendous responsibility and accountability to the Caller and Calling.

Once the Calling of God is made plain to us, it is our spiritual duty to receive the Calling, and place ourselves under the guidance of the Holy Spirit and the human leadership that He chooses. In the same way that we didn't choose our natural parents, nor did we choose Jesus as our Lord and Savior---He chose us---we do not chose what spiritual parents that the Holy Spirit places us under.

Sometimes God chooses a certain individual mentor or group of mentors as in a Bible College. Anyway, we are accountable to be obedient to the Caller, the Call, and our spiritual parents, if we want to grow in Grace and knowledge.

All Christians have a Calling; it may not be Apostle or Prophet but nevertheless it is a legitimate Calling. We cannot escape the responsibility of God's Calling, because it is irrevocable, binding and cannot be rescinded not even by Him.

God will never change His mind on this matter. He is a purpose-driven God who calls purpose-driven people. God sometimes adds to the Calling by broadening it to include other areas of ministry, but not take from it, unless a certain season within the Calling is completed; an addition to the Calling is not a second thought, but a season of the original Calling that we did not yet know about. He will also provide the Spiritual Gifts, finances and support staff necessary to navigate and be effective within the Calling.

God is the same way with Spiritual Gifts; it is the reason that we see Christians who have fallen into some manner of sin but still minister in their Calling with active Spiritual Gifts: God will not cancel the Calling or take the gifts; but He might take the Christian home instead!

Mt. 28.19,20 states: "Go ye therefore and teach all nations....teaching them to observe all things...Mk. 16.17,18 states: "These signs shall follow them that believe; In My Name shall they {meaning us} cast out devils....they shall lay hands on the sick and they shall recover." These verses are associated with the Great Commission; and the Great Commission applies to all Christians.

All Christians have a basic Calling to witness about Jesus Christ. We can invoke and use the Name of Jesus Christ to activate our Spiritual Gifts, to heal the sick, cast out devils or counsel the downtrodden and broken hearted. Being faithful to this basic Calling on our life will advance us, make us available and able for our major life Calling; in that we are faithful in the smaller things, God will advance, promote and propel us into greater things.

As the Apostle Paul recounted his conversion experience to King Agrippa, in Acts 26.13-19, he said "....I was not disobedient unto the heavenly vision." We discover by reading the scriptures, that Paul didn't start out being an Apostle though he had the Calling on his life.

Paul started out as a new convert, a babe in Christ, who needed Ananias to pray for the healing of his blind eyes and activate his destiny. As Paul obeyed the Call, the Holy Spirit led him through many stages of development---the process.

Paul was patient and didn't fight the process, as some of us do, but allowed the process to change him from Saul to Paul; it was more than a mere name change, but a character and personality change---to the mind of Christ Jesus.

Then we see in Acts 13.1: "Now there were in the church what was at Antioch certain prophets and teachers; as Barnabus....and Saul (Paul). Here we see Paul is spoken of as being either (or both) a prophet or teacher, two of the Five-Fold Ministry Ascension Gifts. He was progressing in his Calling.

Paul was elevated to the status of prophet-teacher, when at the end of the meeting, the Holy Spirit spoke audibly: "...separate Me Barnabus and Saul for the work I have called them" (Acts 13.2). The men, who heard the command of the Holy Spirit, laid their hands on Barnabus and Saul: These men where now "sent" ones, and from that day forward were called Apostles: "Which when the apostles, Barnabus and Paul, heard..." (Acts 14.14).

The Holy Spirit promoted them to their high rank in the Body of Christ. For this same reason we should not take it upon ourselves to be called Apostles or Prophets. The Holy Spirit cannot use self-promoted but God-appointed people. This is also a reason why our ministries fail: For one, we are not Called into the particular ministry that we have; and two, we are not prepared, released by the Holy Spirit, and demons overwhelmed us.

"I have finished the course and kept the faith," is what Paul declared in 2 Tim. 4.7. In order to finish the course we have to know what it is! Many of us don't know what our Calling is. The Holy Spirit will reveal it to us if we ask in sincerity--- but once we get the answer we dare not go to Office Depot and have them print up business cards (as many do), but we humbly ask Him what to do next.

As stated earlier, the Holy Spirit will place us under a human mentor; it is not likely that He will teach us personally like He did with Paul, seeing that there are now millions of Spirit-filled Christians around us and in the Body of Christ Body of Christ that He has been using for decades.

Those of us who say, "all I need is Jesus and the King James Version Bible!" Are deceiving ourselves to believe that Jesus doesn't use His human Five-Fold Ministry Ascension Gifts to edify the Body of Christ. He also uses the other saints and Bible translations; plus Jesus didn't speak the King James 1611 English, because in his area Greek, Hebrew, Latin and Aramaic was spoken (however, being God, Jesus could speak any language He need to.).

Jesus Christ, our Commander and Chief, equips us before sending us into battle. The weapons we have are not physical but spiritual and mighty through God to pull down demonic strongholds, expose and uproot a well-entrenched enemy. That is why He places us under a "Commanding Officer," a Ministry Gift.

Many of us miss our Calling because we are too proud to study under someone else. This leads to anger, resentment, rebellion and we even leave the mentor to be free from the appointed authority which is a part of our appointed destiny. The desire to be free from authority, covering, the mentor and his local church, and to start our own ministry, leads us to prematurely call ourselves a "seasoned" Apostle or Prophet(or prophetess), when we haven't completed our training, nor been released by the Holy Spirit. We go along for a season, or even thirty years, until the cycle comes around and we reap what we have sown!

THE DECEPTION OF PRIDE

"The pride of your heart has deceived you..." ---Obad. 1.3

Let us not leave any stone unturned to get to the source of so much wretchedness. Why is it that most of us Christians have no power over sin in our lives? We are not only talking about the leadership falling into disgrace, but the rest of us---maybe not on the evening news---but nevertheless falling short of the glory and expectations of God. We need more power for our Christian Life.

One of the weapons in Satan's arsenal of evil is spiritual pride. Pride is not only one of his weapons, it was the main reason he was thrown out of Heaven. Therefore, pride is a part of his personality; it is very powerful when working in the self-life of human beings. It makes no difference whether the human being is a Christian or not, spiritual pride operates through the Law of Sin and Death, and is a personality defect that has to be dealt with in our Christian Life.

What exactly is deception? Obviously it is the process or state of being deceived. The Webster Dictionary describes it as, "To believe what is false or invalid; to be misled; or to be ensnared; to deliberately misrepresent facts by works or actions in order to further one's own interest; other, beguile, mislead, delude." The biblical example of this phenomenon is recorded in Gen.3.13, where Eve confessed, "The serpent beguiled {(deceived, tricked} me, and I did eat." She was the first human being to be deceived; though in Heaven, the serpent, being Satan, introduced deception to the angelic realm, and was cast out of Heaven because of it: "Satan which deceives the whole world (Rev. 12.9).

Cain was too proud to take even God's advice and rethink his present course of action, and line up with the acceptable Word of God. God told him that a deceiver, the spirit of pride was crouched like a tiger outside his door; it was waiting to devour him; but God counseled Cain not to give in to the evil spirit, but resist it by Faith and confidence in the revealed Word.

However, Cain did not take God seriously, but went out and killed Abel. He ruined his Calling and Commission, his opportunity at ministering to humanity.

There are many ways that a spirit of pride can enter us, but it is first introduced through some type of deception, a single or set of lies, values, postulates, theories, philosophies or beliefs, that we have reckoned as unquestionable truth, and are making important decisions based on them; which means that we gave the spirit of deception control of us and our ministry decisions through this "hook" that this spirit has in our heart.

For example, we may not believe that women can be effective ministers based on what we think of women who have hurt us, or a mother that was, controlling, emotional or mentally unstable. It's not that we hate women, but we don't believe that they are emotionally equipped to handle the demands of pasturing a church and counseling hurting people; and so we come up with this "logical" explanation that seems "biblical" when in fact it's associated with our own pain and is demonic!

The spirit of deception can also opens the door to rebellion, which lets in a spirit of pride, and pride will cause us to be insanely affixed on ourselves, our physical appearance, our finances, our family successes and linage, our vocation, degrees, social and political connections, our material property and vehicles, our stadium-size ministry, and our popularity.

We become more interested in acquiring loyal "fans" than saving souls and mentoring young ministers. Sometimes we are patted on the back by our fans so much that we walk slightly bent over! Yet we are spiritual criminals.

We strut around with our armed body guards when the real enemy is within us; we are the one most hazardous to our health; we are the one toxic to those around us; and we are the one who need to be delivered.

We preach and people throw money at our feet; we are considered "shot-callers" We are on television as a Christian celebrity. We believe our own hype and publicity. We have forgotten where we came from, as sinners, and Who it was who loved and saved us. We are more concerned with selling books, CDs and other merchandise than the sick, seniors, addicts and others in need.

Many of us are terrified to use our fortune and connections to help a struggling minister or ministry, for fear that minister will one day become as prosperous as us, an equal---or worst--- a better minister that us; so we don't help them in order to keep them looking up to us; we make them promises with no intentions of keeping them: "They must remain a fan", we conclude.

In Num. 32.23 warns us that "...your sins shall find you out. Whatever spirit drives us will one day expose us for the person that we really are, that is, the person we have become. It's the duty and nature of evil spirits to deceive and then expose us; as a toaster toast bread because it was manufactured and designed for that purpose, so is the evil spirit of pride bent on exposing us.

The Word in Pro. 16.18 confirms this: "Pride goes before destruction, and a haughty spirit before a fall. And 1 Cor. 10.12 reads:"Wherefore let him who thinks he stands take heed lest he fall." Spiritual pride paralyzes the leadership, and then we the congregation are little more than worshippers of the leader and not true worshippers of Christ. Making flesh our arm to lean on is futile.

If we think that we are all that and a bag of potato chips we are mistaken. If we persist in this type of behavior, the Word says "take heed" because we are about to fall---and hard! Few ministers fully recover their previous status and ministry after a national scandal. God may still use us, but not nearly as much as before. For example, we may go from preaching to 300 million souls worldwide, down to preaching to fifty souls in a small church.

The spirit of pride releases a strange power and counterfeit anointing in the congregation, and we find ourselves deceived into believing that it is the Presence of the Holy Spirit. Even counterfeit prophetic utterances come forth in such a pseudo environment; we become more enslaved, bound to that ministry---not because God told us to stay there--- but because of witchcraft!

Spiritual pride opens the door for other spirits to enter the leader and the congregation; these spirits include religious spirits, lying, greed, jealousy perversion, sickness, disease and other hateful demons.

As deceived leaders we proclaim that "Everything you need is in the house!" We said it to imply that we have all the Spiritual Gifts, spiritual knowledge, wisdom, mantles, divine revelation and counsel. This is a lie. We said it to keep our people from experiencing the fullness of Jesus' manifestations in other ministries; we said it because of insecurity; we want our membership not to give money, time and presence elsewhere; also, as leaders we already know that other ministers in the area have Spiritual Gifts, mantles, teaching and preaching skills that we are envious of, and so we discourages our members from experiencing the power of Christ that blankets the entire Body of Christ.

HOW TO COMBAT THE SPIRIT OF PRIDE

"God resist the proud, but gives grace unto the humble. 7 Submit your selves therefore to God. Resist the devil, and he will flee from you. 8 Draw near to God, and He will draw near to you"---Jam. 34.6,7,8 (KJV).

Humility is the antidote, the key to getting set free from the spirit of pride. If Cain would have humbled himself and listened to God, he would not have stepped out the door and been overwhelmed by the crouched tiger of pride. Humility of self allows the Grace---unmerited favor---and power of God to cleanse the consciousness by the washing and regeneration of the Word.

The Word will cleanse the mind from the demonically imposed sin-consciousness which is under the Law of Sin and Death, that is, a consciousness riddled with condemnation, guilt, shame, regret and other negative emotions---to a righteousness consciousness which is under the Law of the Spirit of Life.

Humility involves our submission to God, our activation of Faith in God and His Word to resist the Devil and his spirit of pride; he will have no legal right or hook in us, and will have to, by the Law of the Spirit of Life, leave us alone.

As we draw near to God he draws near to us too; this decreases the ministry time tremendously, by bridging the gap-time between our distorted mind, and His Christ-Mind, Inner Healing and Deliverance power.

The seeking and obtaining of Inner Healing and Deliverance can be described as this: "Let us draw near with a true heart in full assurance of faith, having our hearts sprinkled from an evil conscious, and our bodies washed with pure water" (Heb. 10.22. Inner Healing and Deliverance is the children's bread!

Notes

CHAPTER EIGHT
ON BENDED KNEES

"Thy Word have I hid in mine heart, that I might not sin against Thee"--- Psalms 119.11 (KJV).

It does not go without mentioning, that we as Christians have a certain amount of "mental ascent" when it comes to the Word of God. We read and understand what the Bible teaches, but do not put that understanding into practice; whereas, the Word of God must be more than a philosophical idea but action; from action to practice, and from practice to a lifestyle.

In the last chapter, we discussed the Calling, Commissioning and how deception and pride can be eliminated through Repentance, Faith and Prayer. But all these must be rooted in the Word of God, to have any lasting effect, because the Holy Spirit only operates by and through the Word of God.

If we wanted to be set free from whatever it is that binds us, what keeps us from living successfully in the Word, the Word of God must be taken seriously. Then we will be successful, prosperous and capable of fulfilling our destiny, the Calling and Commissioning that is on our life.

To begin with, we must be specific and stand on God's Word as the foundation of our thoughts, emotions, will, and imaginations (creativity); and pray according to the Word of God. The best way to pray according to the Word of God is to study the New Covenant, the Word of God as written in the New Testament.

To conquer indwelling demon spirits that have latched onto us like swamp leeches, we must specifically follow the Word of God. In Mt. 4.4, Jesus states, "It is written, Man shall not live by bread alone, but by every word that proceeds out of the mouth of God." Jesus made this statement in response to an attack on His mind, will, emotion and empty, fasted stomach.

Satan tempted Jesus to use His authority solely to validate Himself, to satisfy his stomach, and to learn more about the "mystery" of the "Seed" that had been hidden from him for ages (Col. 1.26)--- prompted the curiosity of Satan. Initially, he wasn't 100% certain that Jesus is the Son of God.

Whereas, Jesus told Him that He was the Son of God because He refused to do what Satan told him! He was the only Man who could resist Satan. Jesus told him that all He was required to do was the will of His Father who sent Him. He wouldn't perform miracles solely for the sake of proving who He is, especially before the one whom he came to destroy the evil works of.

"Then the devil takes Him up into the holy city, and sets Him on the pinnacle of the temple, and says to Him, If you are the Son of God, cast yourself down; for it is written, He shall give His angels charge concerning thee..." (Mt. 4.6,7). This immediately took place after Jesus refused to turn the stones into food. Now, Satan tempted Jesus to put God to a foolish test concerning the Father's love, ability or willingness to protect His Son from imminent danger or death.

"Again, the devil takes Him up into an exceeding high mountain, and shows Him all the kingdoms of the world, and the glory of them. And says unto Him, All these things will I give thee, if thou will fall down and worship me" (V. 8-11).

Jesus' response was most fittingly an example for us. He told the devil to get lost! More King James-like, "get thee hence." The devil took Jesus up on the mountain to show Him the "glory" the pride of owning the whole world, everything and everyone in it. It was pride that Satan wielded before Jesus, the same pride that got him thrown out of Heaven. He boasted of how it was handed to him (by Adam) and that he was in control of it; and all Jesus had to do to get it---NOW---was to bow down and worship him; Jesus didn't dispute his claim.

Many times, as Christians, Satan takes us up and sits us on a high pedestal and promises to give us what our flesh craves---popularity, money, power or sex---if we would bow down and worship him. He is able, via his territorial spirits, to deliver what he promises; but God is also able to deliver the promised judgment upon those of us who live for the devil and die in him---that judgment is Hell.

But the answer to this dilemma lies in Jesus' response: "Thou shall worship the Lord thy God, and Him only shall thou serve" (v.10). The goal of Satan is to get us to worship him; when we fall into sin and stay there, we are worshipping him. The occasional fall is not worship, but the habitual revisiting becomes a habit, then a life-style. The next thing we know we are far away from the narrow road.

And so, as Jesus utilized the Word of God to combat the advances of Satan, we can also use the Word of God to protect, deliver and rescue us from his temptations and traps. When we speak and pray the Word of God, tremendous power is released in our lives, power to destroy yokes and lift burdens.

Because the Word of God is a two-edged sword and our tongue is the member that wields it, we have to be careful that we are not just speaking the Word but doers of it too. If not, the same sword that loops of the heads of demons (figuratively) will loop our head off too! Inasmuch, as we are subject to obey the Word as demons are.

Jesus was (and still is) a Man of Prayer; His life was one of fasting, prayer and fellowship with the Father. He knows the worth of prayer---that it is priceless—and passes this truth on to us. Many times He had to get away from the crowds to spend time with the Father; the people, hungry for the Word, pressed in and thronged Him so that He had little time to eat, pray or even sleep.

Every great manifestation of God's Glory in the Old and New Testament was in response to fervent prayer. Abraham, Moses, David, Solomon, the Prophets and Apostles prayed the glory of God down, and changed their circumstances.

After David committed adultery and murdered Uriah, Bathsheba's husband, he prayed this prayer of godly sorrow and repentance:

1 "Have mercy upon me, O God, according to thy loving kindness; according unto the multitude of thy tender mercies blot out my transgressions. 2 Wash me thoroughly from mine iniquity, and cleanse me from my sin. 3 For I acknowledge my transgressions; and my sin is ever before me. 7 Purge me with hyssop, and I shall be clean; wash me, and I shall be whiter than snow"--- Ps. 51.1-3,7

David is a good example of a man who did some lowdown, scandalous things, but when his head cleared, he realized what he had done and repented. Yet, according to God, David was a man after His own heart! David was human; so are we. And all that God requires when we sin is Repentance and Faith; both of these can be accomplished through humble prayer.

One reason why it is so hard for many of us to pray like David is because we are more sorry that we got caught then we are of the sin. We are reeling from the blow and effects of private or public disgrace than from godly sorrow. Still many of us find it hard to pray because of the spirit of pride saying, "You are pathetic!" And so the spirit of pride won't allow us to pour out our heart to the Lord and ask for forgiveness and cleansing which is also Inner Healing and Deliverance.

This is where the good fight of Faith comes in! If we really want to be delivered we don't care with the demons say or what the people around us think. People don't know what we are going through; they don't know how good God has been to us; they weren't there when He saved our soul; and they weren't there when the rent, light bill, gas bill, phone bill and the car note was due; not to mention they weren't there when the cupboard was bare and our wallet was empty: But God showed up and He delivered us from the trials, tribulations, situations, circumstances, snares, addictions and from criminals!

Saints, God knows what we need to get back on track. In Jn. 16.23, He says to "Ask, Seek and Knock." Having Faith in God we ask for cleansing, Inner Healing and Deliverance; we seek first the Kingdom and its righteousness believing that all the other things we need will be added accordingly.

We speak words impregnated with Faith, what the Word of God says concerning our addictions or weaknesses, and know for certain that we will receive according to our Faith; that God has already blessed us with ALL spiritual blessings in heavenly places and on earth in Christ Jesus (Eph. 1.3). Everything that we will ever need in this journey is provided by our Lord Jesus Christ.

Prayer is the act of "walking by faith and not by sight," as Paul wrote in 2 Cor. 5.7). Knowing that God's Word is true and unchanging, we immediately apply it to our particular problem; we also know that the Word of God is Fact and not a feeling; nor is it the power of the intellect or an act of our will---though we engage our intellect and will in a quality decision to act on the Word of God. Faith comes by hearing, acknowledging and putting into practice the Word of God. It's not putting God to a foolish test when putting Him in remembrance of His promises. It's not that God forgets anything, but quoting His Word back to Him---or out loud in the earth---places a definite time for the fulfillment of that promise, for God who lives in eternity outside of time. We become the point of contact, being both an eternal and finite being where time and eternity meet within our Physical Body. Then God can and will answer the prayer, because He has our permission, our petition or request, the legal right to interfere in our life.

Faith declared, "I have it NOW! Hope declares, "I will have it!" Mental assent declares, "The Word states that I should have it but I don't see it!" Also, mental assent, which is basically human reasoning declares, "I must have sinned (again) and that's why I don't have my petition!"

Lasting Recovery involves genuine Faith; without Faith it is impossible to please God (Heb. 11.6). Do we fully grasp what the word "impossible" means? Neither does Hope please God, though it is the object of our Faith (what we want from God). And mental assent doesn't please God or move His hand to help us.

All mental assent can do is think of reasons why the Word doesn't work for us, or why God is withholding His promises. Mental assent is the mental processes without the input of the human spirit; it is actually the self-life maneuvering to get back on the throne of our life. As it stands, as Born Again Believers, Christ sits on the throne of our life and self is at His feet; the self wants to again be the ruler, with Christ setting at his feet, or out the door!

In the same way that Abraham was fully persuaded that God's promises and His oaths were realities, we must believe: Adhere to, trust in and rely on His promises and His ability and willingness to perform them admirably. This implies not considering the outer situations, circumstances or appearances. But give praise, worship and thanks to God BEFORE the results come---BEFORE the healing, BEFORE the deliverance, and BEFORE the finances arrive.

"Do not fret or have any anxiety about anything, but in every circumstance and in everything, by prayer and petition (definite requests), with thanksgiving, continue to make your wants known to God. 7 And God's peace {shall be yours, that tranquil state of a soul assured of its salvation through Christ, and so fearing nothing from God...} which transcends all understanding shall garrison and mount guard over your hearts and minds in Christ Jesus"---Phil. 4.6 (Amp. Bible).

Faith is believing God's Word; Fear is believing Satan's word. Herein the key to receiving answered prayer: Faith and definite requests to God, believing that we have already received before we actually make the requests. Because we believe that God loves us and already answered our prayer, we rest assured in that tranquil state of praise and worship --- fearing nothing that the demons may bring to slow down or stop our blessing---until we see the manifestation of our prayer. Having peace that transcends all understanding, drives the demons out!

Fearing nothing that comes our way in life is the results of Faith in God; living according to the Word of God goes hand-in-hand with Faith. We cannot have genuine Faith in God and not adhere to, trust in and rely on His revealed Word. Knowing that God cares for us lovingly, affectionately, and watchfully makes it easier to go to Him for Forgiveness, Inner Healing and Deliverance.

Most of us wouldn't confess to anyone we believe would kill us when we are done. And that is what the Devil wants us to think about God. So he tells us to hide our sins, suppress or hide our addictions, indulgences, urges and thinking distortions instead of getting help. Then one day he springs the trap and the whole world knows what we have been doing more or less all of our life!

Jos. 1.8 advises us not to let the Word of God depart from our mouth; and the only way it will be in the mouth is that it first be abundantly in the heart; for out of the abundance of the heart {human spirit's intuition, intellect, emotions, will, imagination} the mouth will speak. Then we'll experience soul prosperity. Praying according to the Word, which is hidden in our heart, keeps us from habitual sin.

Another great principle to consider is written in Mat. 18.18 (Amp. Bible). "Truly I tell you, whatever you forbid and declare to be improper and unlawful on earth must be what is already forbidden in heaven, and whatever you permit and declare proper and lawful on earth must be what is already permitted in heaven."

The Standard for what is unlawful or improper is in relation to the Word of God. Evil, the entire works of Satan has been declared unlawful everywhere except in Hell. When we pray the perfect will of God "Thy will be done in earth as it is in heaven," we are requesting that the same Standard be invoked here on earth that is the Spiritual Law and legal state environment in Heaven.

For example: There is no sicknesses, diseases, addictions or criminal activity in heaven, and so we can declare and decree ourselves legally free (as the fruit of Salvation) of all of these bondages on earth.

And the second part of the verse affirms the legal status of Heaven with our free will to declare and decree freedom according to the Spiritual Law of the Spirit of Life, the legal state of Heaven that is free from evil and its consequences. For whom the Son of God has set free is free indeed!

Addictions know no boundaries: Age, race, gender, social status, the Saved and un-Saved fall victim to drugs, alcohol, tobacco, sexual addictions, and deviant, antisocial behaviors. However, we as Christians have a resource available that others do not have: A Covenant relationship with God. It is a matter of if we want to remain a Victim or achieve Victory. Because God can turn a mess into a message, a test into a testimony, a trial into a triumph, and a victim into a victory.

Sometimes we think that God is going to do everything for us, that He can somehow "force us" to follow the Word. But that is not the truth. God did not force us to get Saved nor will He force us to stay Saved. God, through Jesus Christ and the Holy Spirit are Covenant Partners with us.

As Partners, the Trinity will not and cannot do all of the work; we have to purposely engage our will and cooperate with our Partners. And as the Three are One in Spirit, we don't have to satisfy three different Persons, but One. Nevertheless, we pray to the Father in Jesus' Name because He told us too.

Mat. 18.19 (Amp. Bible) concludes and establishes that the action must began with us, on earth, and not in Heaven at the throne of God: "Again I tell you, if two of you on earth agree (harmonize together, make a symphony together) about whatever {any-thing and everything} they may ask, it will come to pass and be done for them by My Father in heaven." Two or more Christians in agreement can turn the table on the Devil and erase a multitude of sins.

Herein lies the authority and power of the Believer to destroy yokes and lift heavy burdens. Hiding our sins isn't the answer; it is like a closet full of filthy clothes that as time passes stinks up the whole house; or worst, a refrigerator, that has been turned off for months but full of raw meat, then opened! Getting sins forgiven, washed away and their outworking consequences made none and void is the ideal goal. Therefore, we come into agreement with one another, bind the demonic spirits responsible for the sicknesses or addictions on earth, and God in Heaven honors our decisions and causes them to be tangible in our life.

God knows what we have need of before we ask; nevertheless, we have to ask in order that He may enter into our life. Ask and you shall receive, is what Jesus taught; also, have Faith in God, or have the Faith of God by speaking positive words of Faith, and call those things that be not as yet as though they already exist in the natural realm.

Walking by Faith and not by sight is what we are talking about. If we believe that God's Word is true we have to live by it. This will cause our Faith to grow from the mustard seed kind to the great Faith that Jesus spoke of concerning the Roman centurion.

Though everyone has been dealt a measure of Faith in order to get Saved in the first place, not everyone uses their Faith to get Saved, but use it to follow other religions and philosophies; but Faith increases by hearing, acknowledging and putting into practice---everyday use---the Word of God.

Fear creates doubt: Doubt comes by hearing and practicing unbelief, false religions and philosophies. So we have to practice being positive in our thinking and don't give up on ourselves or recovery. This is done by praying the solution and not complaining to God, ourselves or to friends about the problem. Every thought or action must mirror and confirm what we believe God for. Being vigilant, lest a negative mental image of failure stay in the conscious mind too long and become a permanent fixture!

If doubt, which is a vain imagination comes into the mind, rebuke it, and it will burst like a bubble. Summit to God, resist the Devil and he will flee (Jam. 4.7).

"Because when they knew and recognized Him as God, they did not honor and glorify Him as God or give Him thanks. But instead they became futile and godless in their thinking {with vain imagining, foolish reasoning and stupid speculations} and their senseless minds were darkened. 22 Claiming to be wise, they became fools..."---Ro. 1.21,22 (Amp. Bible).

The imagination is the facility of the soul that is capable of conceiving and grasping abstract ideas, concepts, theories and principles. It enables us to plan today for a possible tomorrow (which is not promised to any of us). The imagination is also the facility of the soul that can create art, literature, music, build and construct things that have never existed before; it is also the facility that we use to dream at night, daydream or fantasize.

But imagination corrupted by the flesh, world or demons, becomes the facility used to create paranoia—fearful, terrifying and paralyzing thoughts that people are after us to do harm when they are not; it also creates doubt, unbelief, religious error, racism, sexual fantasy, lust, pride, vanity, self-importance and self-righteousness; these are examples of vain imaginations.

Vain imaginations are often projected into our minds by the territorial spirits; often it is done during the sleep state, meditations or daydreaming period when the mind is idle and open. Certain Eastern meditation techniques relax the mind as to become vulnerable to psychic attacks from demons.

God has imagination too; His is called divine imaginations. Through His facility He sends us what we call visions and dreams. This is one of God's primary methods of communication. Divine imaginations is God sending us mental images (pictures) of our future or visual information about others; He also sends us visual information about local or world situations and circumstances, our destiny and

Calling, His plans, purposes and pursuits using us or just the overall plan; He also sends visions of Himself so that we can personally know Him.

The mind of God is like a television station. He sends out powerful visual images with an audible tract containing information about who He is, and His plans. These images may be real time or future; and since God always is in the present, He knows what is destined to happen throughout human history. Those who are sensitive and close to God see visions from God; God is no respecter of persons; He will talk to anyone who will listen!

"Be well balanced (temperate, sober of mind), be vigilant and cautious at all times; for that enemy of yours, the devil, roams around like a lion roaring {in fierce hunger}, seeking someone to seize upon and devour. 9 Withstand him; be firm in faith..."---1 Pet. 5.8, 9 (Amp. Bible).

The biggest deception that Satan has pulled off since the Garden of Eden is to convince humanity that he doesn't exist. The Word of God declares that there is such a person as Satan or the Devil, and that he is alive and living on Earth. He is not as powerful as he was before Calvary, since the decisive victory won by Jesus Christ, but he still remains the most notorious murderer, liar and trickster that has even lived. But those who are In Christ Jesus, have weapons to fight against this entity. Knowing this, we are not ignorant of his devices and tactics.

Satan moves and maneuvers in the Psychic or Mental Realm, the realm of the senses; he also uses subtle suggestions, deceptions and delusions. One thing for sure, his implanted thoughts do not line up with the Word of God and can be easily discerned by those of us who diligently study the Bible. But, during the years when we didn't know the Word of God, was when Satan got his foothold.

Now we have to be more conscious of our thought processes, motives, desires and reasoning to make sure we are not being lured into one of his traps. We have to cast down and reject dreams, visions, false prophecies or personal feelings that don't line up with the Word. We also have to practice resisting the "doubting Thomas'" of the local churches and the secular world.

As doubting Thomas' we sound so knowledgeable when we say: "Once an alcoholic, always an alcoholic, or "Once a drug addict, always a drug addict"---which is NOT the Word of God concerning New Creatures in Christ Jesus; this thinking distortion is also extended to other moral failures as a reason not to help fallen Christians get back on their feet; it is also proclaiming that the Blood of Jesus Christ is powerless to deliver addicts or certain people, there-fore doubting the effectiveness of the Word of God. And so we would rather use this excuse to shoot the fallen Christians like injured horses!

Jesus Christ took upon Himself our grief, sicknesses, weaknesses and distresses, even the pains and consequences of punishment, and with the stripes that wounded Him we are healed and made whole (Isa. 53.4). In so doing, He not only secured eternal Salvation for those who believe in him, but Healing and Deliverance from the molestation of unclean spirits.

That is why the weapons of our warfare are not physical weapons, but mighty and effective to demolish strongholds of every kind; there is no bondage that the Holy Spirit cannot break; and the only person that He cannot save is the one who doesn't want to get Saved.

For the most part, thoughts are formed in the brain by observation, association, and teaching. Though it is difficult to avoid hearing other people's opinions, we can never-theless avoid soul ties with them, certain places, programs and reading printed materials that is contrary to Christian belief, that doesn't support our confession of Faith, Healing and Deliverance goals.

Face it, if we want to stop drinking we have to stop buying liquor, going to bars and clubs and hanging out with people who drink! Why? Because we are saying one thing and doing another; we are not making arrangements to stop but to continue drinking. This principle applies to all addictions, strongholds, habits or thinking distortions: Feed your Faith and starve your Doubts to death! Whatever you feed will get the fattest; whatever you starve will eventually die.

Thinking positively is not a new idea. Non-Christian motivational speakers have capitalized on this concept, and perhaps have helped a lot of depressed people; they have also created a lot of multimillion and billionaires too.

But positive thinking alone will not change the core of us, though it will alter many thinking patterns. Here is where the Word of God and prayer comes in, the help of the powerful, life-changing Holy Spirit. Not letting the Word depart from before our eyes and heart is the key to confessing the truth in the earth about who we are, and the positive confession of our destiny with our mouth. And God will make His Word good if we diligently act upon it as we should.

We make every prayer a confession of Faith, and don't undo those prayers by listening to the "speculations," the vain imaginations of our mind whose goal is to return to the familiar, that former state of pleasure and freedom from God, that state of thinking that it's okay to sin as long as it's temporary; or, "I'm Saved, so I can sin and not lose my Salvation… or I am the Bishop, and so…"

We pray to the Father in the Name of Jesus (Jn. 16.23) because there isn't another way to approach God and be accepted by Him. Because of our confidence in Jesus, the Father answers and grants our petitions.

Our praying authority comes from Jesus, the High Priest of the Heavenly Sanctuary (Acts 3.12). Without the use of His Name, we are stuck, like other religions, with a form of godliness without the actual relationship and power to overcome adversity---mainly, our adversary the Devil, and our wicked desires to please our flesh. Prayer is planting the seed of Faith to claim our harvest!

TYPES OF PRAYERS

There are many types of prayers and ways to pray; and since this is not a book on prayer only, we will only discuss a few types of prayer.

The Prayer of Faith is described in many ways and places in the New Testament. Prayer for the Christian is based on the New Testament Covenant. We should not pray like David prayed under the Old Testament Covenant of Law---that God would kill our enemies. But under Grace there is forgiveness and mercy.

In Mk. 11.24 it states, "Therefore I tell you, whatever you ask for in prayer, believe that you have received it, and it will be yours." Jesus proclaimed, "Have Faith in God." Another translation says, "Have the Faith of God," which also makes sense because God does everything through the exercise of His Faith. He has dealt to everyone a measure, a degree, a mustard seed of His divine Faith. God, through Faith, calls those things that be not as though they already were; this is the Prayer based and rooted in Faith---to call those things that be not as yet as though they already exist.

In Eph. 6.10-17, the Apostle Paul gave a discourse on spiritual warfare. From there he immediately wrote of prayer being an essential part of that spiritual warfare: "Pray at all times (on every occasion, in every season) in the Spirit, with all {manner of} prayer and entreaty"--- Eph 6.18 (Amp. Bible).

The Prayer of Consecration is another type of prayer that is widely described and used in the New Testament Covenant. To consecrate means to sanctify, separate for a divine purpose. We as Christians are a people set aside by God. We are members of His divine family, the Church, the Bride of Christ, the fruit, being the children of the Resurrection. Therefore, we are separated from the world, and do separate ourselves by uttering this type of prayer. We declare and decree aloud that we belong to Christ and He belongs to us!

In the upper room, Jesus consecrated the wine and the bread through prayer. "And as they were eating, Jesus took bread, and blessed it, and brake it, and gave it to the disciples, and said, "Take, eat, this is my body. And He took the cup, and gave thanks, and gave it to them, saying, Drink ye all of it. For this is my blood of the New Testament" (Mat. 28.26-28).

In Jn. 17.15-17 (Amp. Bible), Jesus consecrated, set apart disciples for a special purpose: "I do not ask that You take them out of the world, but that You will keep and protect them from the evil one. They are not of the world (worldly, belonging to the world), {just} as I am not of the world. Sanctify them {purify, consecrate, separate them for Yourself, make them holy} by the Truth; Your word is Truth."

In further verses, Jesus consecrated Himself and future Believers in the Body of Christ, so that we are also sanctified, purified, separated and wholly consecrated to and In Him. In the same way the Father sent Jesus into the world,

Jesus sends us into the world with the same consecration through prayer.

Prayer of Commitment: "Delight yourself also in the Lord, and He will give you the desires and secret petitions of your heart. Commit your ways to the Lord {roll and repose each care of your load on Him}; trust (lean on, rely on, and be confident) also in Him and He will bring it to pass" (Ps. 37.4,5 Amp. Bible). It is obvious that the Prayer of Commitment involves our spiritual relationship with God. It is our commitment to Him, not His commitment to us that is involved. God is faithful; and we are not always faithful, though we try with all our might.

Many times are burdens are so heavy that we cannot lift them; that is when we roll or drag them to the cross. Then there are times when out burdens are so heavy that we have not the strength to roll or drag them; that is when we seek out a prayer partner, a Christian to stand in agreement and believe with us, that what we ask, believing that we have already received, will materialize according to our Faith in the Word of God.

Peter wrote, "Casting the whole of your cares {all you anxieties, all your worries. All your concerns, once and for all} on Him; for He cares for you affectionately and cares about you watchfully" (1 Pet. 5.7 Amp. Bible). This is saying a lot about our New Testament Covenant; how God is available and willing to accept our burdens as His own and either help us to carry them or eliminate them altogether. Prayer is the key to getting supernatural help in this natural world; having God in our world when the world is more or less God-less.

Jesus affirmed this when speaking to the disciples concerning the Battle of Life: "Therefore I say to you, do not worry about your life, what you will eat; or about your body, what you will wear. But seek His kingdom, and these things will be given to you as well" (Lk. 12.22,31).

Knowing this truth frees us from the anxiety (fear) of worrying about finances, health, marriage and the host of other concerns we have as human being living in a materialistic world. God knows that we don't live in a cave; He knows we need a certain amount of money to survive on, and so He says commit our ways to Him and he will take care of us.

"For he that speaks in an unknown tongue, speaks not unto men, but unto God; for no man understands him, howbeit in the Spirit he speaks mysteries." 1 "But you, beloved, building up yourself on your most holy faith, praying in the Holy Ghost"---1 Cor. 14.4 Jude 1.20 (KJV).

Praying in Tongues is the last type of prayer to be discussed in this chapter. This phenomenon is strictly a New Testament manifestation of the Holy Spirit. Over the years there has been much controversy concerning the Baptism in/with the Holy Spirit, accompanied by the scriptural evidence of speaking in other/ unknown tongues (Acts.2.4).

The Baptism in the Holy Spirit is a second work of Grace through Faith. It was made possible for Believers to receive this gift on the day of Pentecost---fifty days after the crucifixion of the Lord Jesus Christ. Further evidence that we have been Baptized in the Holy Spirit is the manifestation of one or several of the nine Spiritual Gifts: Tongues, Interpretation of Tongues, Discerning of Spirits, Prophecy, Word of Wisdom, Word of Knowledge, Gifts of Healing, Working of Miracles, and the Gift of Faith (1 Cor. 12.7-11).

The difference between the Baptism in the Holy Spirit and Salvation, is that Salvation/Regeneration involves the indwelling and residence of the Holy Spirit within our human spirit causing a spiritual awakening and Eternal Life; whereas, the Baptism in the Holy Spirit is power for service.

We can therefore be Saved without the Baptism in the Holy Spirit; but we cannot be un-Saved and Baptized in the Holy Spirit. In order to qualify to receive the second work of Grace, the first work of Grace, Salvation must be accomplished. There are many New Testament examples where the Believer received both apparently at the same time; but in the Word of God, Salvation took first place even if it was only by a second.

Again, the manifestations of Spiritual Gifts or the Baptism in the Holy Spirit is not an evidence of integrity or Christian moral character; it's only that God---who is no respecter of persons---chose us as a vessel to accomplish some task for Him; and of course, He did the choosing before the foundation of the world. **The true evidence of Salvation is a changed life!**

The benefits to those of us Christians who are Baptized in the Holy Spirit is our increased power and awareness of who we are in Christ, and our ability to talk to the Father, Son or Holy Spirit, and speak mysteries into the natural world, in a language that cannot be twisted or corrupted by our flesh, unclean spirits that may be hidden deep within our soul (intellect, emotions, will, imagination), or those assigned to curse, hinder, tempt, destroy or monitor us.

Unclean spirits can create delusions and a blocking action to keep us from asking or receiving the help of God. They can deceive us into thinking that we are okay, and the Word concerning the renewing of the mind is for other Christians who need it more than we do, that everyone else is wrong; it also can be we are led to believe that no one will ever discover what we are doing.

But praying in the Spirit is supernatural and the territorial spirits or indwelling spirits don't know what we are praying about (they lost their ability to interpret this spiritual language). But in our daily dialect---since demons have been on the earth before the Garden of Eden---they can understand and fluently speak every language that was ever spoken on earth; but they cannot interpret the Language of the Spirit of Life, the "original" language of God and the holy angels.

Apostle Paul and Apostle Jude wrote that speaking in tongues edifies, builds us up spiritually (1 Cor. 14.4 Jude 1.20). There is yoke-destroying, devil-stomping power in praying in Tongues. "For if I pray in an unknown tongue, my spirit prays, but my understanding is unfruitful" (1 Cor. 14.14). This states that we are also strengthened and build up where we are weak, but this is done independently of the intellect, emotions, will and imagination, and there-fore cannot be influenced by us or the demonic powers. This is available power for living in Christ.

The speaking in Tongues is the Holy Spirit talking or praying from His residence in us. And though we are Saved without this Baptism, and have the Person of the Holy Spirit in us, He has not been given our permission to use our mouth to speak into our life, and to speak the perfect will of God into the earth. We gave Him permission to indwell us and live, but not permission to speak out of our mouth the perfect will of God as He deems (not us) necessary, and at His appropriate timing. This is something to seriously think about!

The Baptism in the Holy Spirit is vital to getting set free on the inside and outside---declaring the Word of God, decree-ing the Word of God, and taking spiritual authority through the Word of God by praying in the Holy Spirit. The Baptism in the Holy Spirit tongues can also be prayed corporately, that is, the entire church can pray aloud together (This is not preaching in Tongues which is forbidden because no one knows what is being said); or the Gift of Tongues can be uttered as long as someone immediately interprets it (1 Cor. 14). The Baptism in the Holy Spirit is a must for Christians to fight a winning Battle of Life and **Battle For Life**.

How do we as Christians get Baptized in the Holy Spirit? Here is a clue: John the Baptist declared: "But He that sent me to baptize with water, the same said unto me. Upon whom you shall see the Spirit descending, and remain on Him, the same is He which baptizes with the Holy Ghost" (Jn. 1.33). So we see through scriptural reference, the Person John was referring to is Jesus Christ; He is the One who Baptizes us in the Holy Spirit, for He is also the one who sent the Holy Spirit back to the natural realm to continue His work of Redemption.

The Baptism in the Holy Spirit---a gift received by Faith---can be received by direct prayer or laying on of hands by any Christian who is also Baptized in the Holy Spirit. Often, after Inner Healing and Deliverance has taken place, the Baptism in the Holy Spirit is easier to receive.

DELIVERANCE PRAYER

Heavenly Father, I humble myself before You in the Name of Jesus Christ. I confess my sins; I am sorry for every one of them. I have accepted Jesus Christ as my Lord and Savior. I am redeemed by the Blood of Jesus and entitled to Inner Healing and Deliverance. Lord, through the power of the Holy Spirit, cleanse me. I have unwisely allowed (Name the unclean spirit(s) to gain access, oppress, torment and use me. I seek to recover my freedom, wholeness, and to exercise free will over my spirit, soul, mental facilities, will, intellect, emotions, imagination and physical body, to be set free of all infirmities and influences of unclean spirits.

I denounce Satan and his plans, purposes, and pursuits. I separate myself from Satan and claim refuge in the Lord Jesus Christ. I demand and decree my immediate release from all evil spirits and influences operating in my life. In Jesus' Name, I exercise my will and Christian Authority over evil spirits assigned to harass, steal, kill and destroy me. I bind and break your power, strongholds, thinking distortions, delusions, addictions and influences in the Name of Jesus.

BY FAITH: In the Name of Jesus Christ, I NOW declare that you unclean spirits are unlawfully encroaching according to the Word of God: I demand that you leave me! I am a child of God. I declare: Depart from me you cursed spirits!

BY FAITH: I claim the promises: (Joel 2.32) "That whosoever shall call upon the Name of the Lord shall be delivered." The Word cleanses me from all sin. I am a holy temple of God; and Greater is He within me than he that is in the world. I belong to Christ and Him only will I serve. Lord Jesus Christ, right NOW, I accept my Deliverance. Fill me, Lord, with your Holy Spirit. O bless the Name of Jesus. Amen!

PRAYER OF DOMINION

Father, in the Name of Jesus, I take spiritual authority against the Principalities, Powers, Rulers of the Darkness and Spiritual Wickedness in the heavenly places assigned to this region. I exercise dominion against all demonic manipulations, control, influences and strongholds. I declare them to be unlawfully assembled according to the Word of God. Therefore in the Name and by the Blood of Jesus, I render their works bound in the earth as they are in Heaven. In Jesus' Name,

I openly declare that every manifestation, operation, assignment or maneuver of the enemy has become ineffective and made void. I exercise dominion against all evil spirits assigned to steal, kill and destroy this people. In the Name and by the Blood of Jesus Christ, I bind all unclean spirits, including tormenting, perversion, lying, prejudice, racism, anger, hatred, un-forgiveness, rebellion, religion, legalism, condemnation, guilt, inferiority, rejection, greed, drug dealing, drug and alcohol addictions, violence, child abuse, domestic violence, pornography, sexual perversions, sin, sicknesses, diseases, poverty---plus every spirit that binds and oppresses this people.

BY NOW FAITH, I activate the Blood of Jesus over this region and over this people. I declare the Blood to be a witness against the territorial spirit activity and their eternal defeat. I now release this people in the Name of Jesus from all bondages and pronounce them free to serve the Lord Jesus Christ.

BY NOW FAITH, I declare the people blessed and open to the Spirit of God, sensitive to the voice of the Holy Spirit, the Word and the will of God. I decree that where sin abounds that Grace much more abounds, that the Life and Light of Christ prevails against the darkness of Satan, that truth prevails against deception; Deliverance prevails against bondage, and obedience prevails against rebellion. Father, I thank and praise You that Your Kingdom has come and Your will is being done in the earth as it is in Heaven.

I declare in the Name of Jesus that this region is holy ground and consecrated to Your purpose. Holy Spirit, fall upon this region and make Your Presence known, that the will of God be enforced by the Church. To Jesus be honor and glory forever, amen.

Notes

CHAPTER NINE
THE UNDISCOVERED COUNTRY

"And he shall speak great words against the Most High, and shall wear out the saints of the Most High..."---Dan. 7.25 (KJV).

These are undoubtedly the years of Restitution and New Beginnings. Those who embrace this paradigm shift that has taken place in the Spirit Realm must be particularly careful as not to allow the enemy to steal our time!

We all, being mortals, have a certain amount of time to live, and therefore a limited amount of time to do what God has called us to do. Satan and the territorial spirits will attempt to persuade us to invest our limited time and resources in the sensual world of pleasure, entertainment and other worldly endeavors, and not be Born Again, or enter into our appointed destiny, and subsequently not finish the course with joy.

Time is our valuable asset; seasons are window opportunities placed in time. If we miss the time we also miss the season. Satan's end-time strategy is to wear out the saints of God. Since he was defeated by Jesus Christ at Calvary, his strategy is to mentally and physically wear us out through futile behaviors, wasted motions and fleshly acts of service---be they religious or secular. The motive is to scatter our attention from the true plan and purpose of God in our life and waste precious time, whereby we leave out of this world tired, worn out, disappointed, disgusted, unsatisfied and defeated.

Time Wasters are demon spirits, but they create and operate through distractions. Distractions manifest as people, events, situations and circumstances that take our focus off of Christ, the Christian Purpose and destiny that God has predestined, prepared and appointed us for.

In the **Battle For Life**, we have to be careful if we are to acquire and maintain our Inner Healing and Deliverance. Even in the local churches are many haters; we all know this group or class of Christian---people who don't want to see us prosper. If it were advantageous to plan a Hater's Convention, the extraordinary task would be to find a building large enough to hold so many Haters; or perhaps a large island should be leased? Then, there is always the possibility that no one would come to the Hater's Convention because, of course, they hate each other too!

The haters are the Christian Soldiers who shoot to death their own wounded comrades; who will not lift a finger to support a fallen brother, sister or pastor, but are quick to stand over us and administer the coup de grace. Beware of them: They are one of the most lethal weapons in Satan's arsenal.

When we are enjoying our peace and recovery from drugs, alcohol or a sexual morality fall, here they come to forever hold our failure (s) over our head, saying "I am so disappointed in you---how could you have done such a thing! I will never trust you again!" They are Time Wasters.

There are almost endless ways to waste our precious time here on earth. A cause that appears on the surface to be good, necessary and noble, could actually tie us up and keep us from being used by God, when the position could be adequately filled by someone who doesn't want to serve God anyway.

Sometimes, a spirit of "false burden" leads us (deceives us by playing on our emotions, feelings or sense of wanting to see change) to believe that no one can do the job but us; we must sit on the committee at the school board, hospital, city council or even a church-run board. But if after consulting God we do not receive the "go"---leave it alone; for us, it is a Time Waster, though it may be a legitimate cause and worthy of being done---but not by us! We must redeem the times because the days are numbered and extremely evil.

The Undiscovered Country is similar to the new world that the Europeans arrive in during the 1600. They risked their lives to venture to the new world, and many of them were buried during the harsh winter. But as soon as the winter was over, they pressed further inland to discover the rest of the country. The Undiscovered Country is that territory within us that we have not known, neither have we explored; for we have not come this way before. The Undiscovered Country is also the New Creature in Christ Jesus, the part of us whom we have to be acquainted with, embrace, love, obey and appreciate, though we know a whole lot about the old creature.

Many philosophers have expounded on this concept by proclaiming, "Know thyself!" Some refer to the old creature we were as the dark side of the soul, or the part of all of us we keep hidden out of sight, suppressed and under lock and key, less he gets out publicly and ruins our entire life. And so, we wear all types of masks and costumes because life is a Broadway production. Therefore, in order to know thyself we have to study thyself.

The Undiscovered Country is the part of us that if there was no law or punishment for wrongdoing, we would do almost any-thing! It is our deepest, darkest, best-kept secrets that if anyone found out, they would be appalled. It is that part of us that even God said was desperately wicked.

In counseling those incarcerated in prison, it was discovered that the majority of those convicted of heinous crimes including serial murders, never thought that they were capable of such acts. Even their family members, neighbors and school teachers were shocked to hear of the news. "He was so gifted and polite!" Others said, said, "He was so quiet!" His pastor added: "He was in church every Sunday!" But, of course, they were all deceived concerning what was really in that person's heart.

We should never say what we will not do; if it were not for the Grace of God that we are in our right mind (some of us) we would be in prison, a mental institution, homeless or on Death Row with the hundreds of men and women awaiting execution all over the country.

And so it is with the Christians who have fallen. What is needed most is we that are spiritual to help them get back on their feet---not to constantly remind them of the fall, and burn the forever banded on the forehead: SINNER! And more often than not the church aligns in agreement with the world and not the Word of God concerning Repentance and Faith. The world does not believe that people can permanently change because repentance or a "Born Again" experience.

It's interesting how certain Christians, the Haters believe that the Blood of Jesus Christ is capable of taking away their sins but not anyone else's sins. It is the double standard in the local church. This type of thinking devalues the Blood of Jesus, and groups it with other religious "phrases". When we ask a Christian, "How are you doing?" The usual response is, "Blessed." Which is eternally true, but doesn't provide us any useful information to get to know them. They are wearing the "Christian Mask," pretending that they have no problems, struggles, or need prayer or wise counsel for anything.

The devaluing of the power of the Blood causes us to discount the Blood as Atonement for sins of the fallen Christian. The exercise of Faith necessary to invoke the release of cleansing, does not happen because the Blood of Jesus has become a mental and religious concept, and not a Faith-based reality.

Therefore, many churches have stopped singing songs about the Blood of Jesus because it sounds gross to them (the Blood being made common as human or animal blood). So when Christians fall, the response is ridicule, separation or excommunication, "silencing" as the Baptists call it.

God, who knows and is the Way, Truth, and Life said: "The heart is deceitful above all things, and it is exceedingly perverse and corrupt and severely, mortally sick! Who can know it {perceive, understand, be acquainted with his own heart and mind}"---Jer. 17.9 (Amp. Bible).

The King James Version describes the heart as "desperately wicked". The idea is the same: Without the Grace and help of God we might do anything!

The Undiscovered Country is also the place where demonic spirits hide. They hide here because it is the least likely place for us look---be aware of their presence. From the comfortable council room, they pull the strings that make us jump and do weird things---that please them.

So, we have to be aware of Seemingly Unimportant Decisions (SUD). When we are not using our minds, being passive or practicing Transcendental Meditation, Yoga, or other Eastern "enlightening" disciplines, we are more open to suggestions than we were if we were using the functions of our mind to think.

When we empty the mind of relevant thoughts and feelings, or cease to monitor our thoughts, feelings and emotions, we enter into the Undiscovered Country. And like the "default" setting and subprogram on a computer that returns when it has lost track of what it is doing, we return and lean on the familiar arm of the flesh; there, the demons are waiting to get control of our life; and the SUD thought is likely the one that leads us in the direction to sin; because it will be the one that come out of us so powerfully; nevertheless, we will know it for what it is because it will NEVER pass the test of the Word of God!

Many of us have fallen into sin or ill situation because of that Seemingly Unimportant Decision. It could be visiting an ex-girlfriend when we are married; or going to the store in the middle of the night and get raped or robbed! On that note, thousands of people are in prison because of the sudden urge to go someplace or do something uncharacteristic of their previous behavior.

VAIN IMAGINATIONS

"Casting down imaginations...and bringing into captivity every thought to the obedience of Christ"--- 2 Cor. 10.5 (KJV.)

Thoughts + Feelings +Emotions = Behaviors. As stated earlier, there is such a thing as the imagination being out of phase with the rest of the mind, including the intellect. A Christian must guard against recurring thoughts that belong to the old man or demons, who will use these thoughts to regain his former position; and the spirits that are associated with the old man will definitely use the flesh, the self-life and the Law of Sin and Death to regain control.

DEMONIC INTERFERENCE

Although there are hundreds of symptoms of demonic interference, some of which have their root in emotional and medical disorders that may be chemical or electrical related, a physician should always be consulted. As these lists are only a guideline to recognizing problems, it is not meant to be conclusive or a substitute for medical attention: Fail to get breakthrough after much fasting and prayers, unexplained illness with no diagnosis, including rashes, practicing the Occult (including witchcraft and Ouija board), repeated backsliding in the same area, chronic depression, suicide attempts, eating disorders, hostile behavior, unexplained sulfur-like odor, seizures, suddenly compelled to go places, cutting the flesh, excessive compulsive behaviors, difficulty reading Bible, difficulty worshipping, difficulty repenting, mental ill-nesses (all types), hearing voices, mocking the

Word of God and/or servants of God, cursing God or Jesus, superhuman strength, terror in the mind, recurring nightmares, combat flashbacks, seeing evil spirits, actual visitation by evil spirits.

Jesus is the Great Physician. He said, "Ask and you shall receive. It is always to our best interest to do what Jesus says. But often times, we find it all but impossible to obey His Word. These are times when the influences of the demonic kingdom, family, friends and religious folks are at their worst in our lives.

It is beneficial to our spiritual growth to be find a trusted, dedicated, non-judgmental professional to get help; a ministry empowered by the Holy Spirit and devoted to setting the captives free, is what's needed; not a gossiper or busybody. We should pray and ask God to direct us to someone whom He uses to release and activate Physical Healing, Emotional Healing, Deliverance and Restoration, to whomever calls upon the Name of the Lord.

What Do You Seek Healing And Deliverance For?

We as Christians are required to live by the Standard of the Word of God. The Christian denominations, the Constitution and the legal system even adds a little more to that. Christians are to live a life above reproach and blame. Many of us strive daily to live up to these standards; sometimes we are trusting in God, other times we are maintaining a façade, the appearance of living holy---going through the motions--- when in fact we are only suppressing the manifestations of our urges, fantasies and desires. But even the smallest volcano will someday blow, and the destruction in its wake can be most devastating to those around it.

The Undiscovered Country deep within us is full of active and dormant volcanoes: Some small and others humongous. Many have erupted and spent their fury and now lain dormant. But there are many more potential disasters lurking deep below the surface. Under the right conditions they will bust loose with a fury that would be impossible for us to contain; impatience turns into irritation; irritation into anger; anger into rage; rage into violence; violence into murder; murder into imprisonment; imprisonment into State Execution.

Secret sins are not volcanoes but the effect are the same. Those urges that we suppress, fail to suppress and indulge in behind closed doors will be discovered.

The Undiscovered Country can be a very crowded place, a place that we seldom visit to clean house, but the occupants seem to come and go as they please! This is the place the Holy Spirit goes in and cleans house; He heals the hurts and soothes the pains; this is where He restores the fractured personality---having been fractured during the Battle of Life and **The Battle For Life**.

Our personality was fractured by our own sins and lifestyle plus the deeds of familiar and territorial spirits. This was also added to by family and social pressures, abuse and betrayals; this is also where the Love of Christ rushes in like a mighty wind and sweeps away the entrenched spirits who have been dictating to us their will and sometimes even our will--- because, at times, we enjoyed sinning!

Even in a court of law, "the devil made me do it," Is not an accepted defense! We are responsible to God for the vain imaginations that lead us into actions that jeopardize our entire being; spirit, soul, natural body and freedom, even though we may have been coerced to do evil.

The legacy of the true Christian is not we never fall, but if we fall we have Jesus Christ and the other brethren to help us get back up.

Many Heavy Weight Boxing champions have been knocked down, only to return in the later rounds to win. So it is with us; we may be down at times but we get back up before the bell rings and the fight is over.

Inner Healing takes place when we pour out our heart to God; we empty ourselves of our own plans, hopes, ambitions, pride and self-sufficiency and ask God to search our entire heart, the deepest recesses and territory within the Undiscovered Country, to bind up our broken heart and comfort our morning, and provide the oil of gladness, a garment of praise instead of the spirit of discouragement and despair; to drive out the enemy and set fire to his camp---the fire of the Holy Ghost---and set us at liberty, who have been bruised and misused.

The healing of past hurts and bruised emotions will effect a lasting change in the way we think. The renewing of the mind and the balancing of the intellect, emotions, will and imagination will also happen; the removal of unclean spirits, strongholds, delusions, vain imaginations, thinking distortions and the territorial spirit control that we believed as truth will be revealed for what they are----lies! Before we know it, the mind will quiet and have less background chatter going on (demons are gone, no more board meetings). And we will be able to sleep soundly, awaken refreshed, and have a closer, intimate relationship with God.

Let us not be like King Saul, who in his last days came to this conclusion: "I have played the fool, and have erred exceedingly!"--- 1 Sam. 26.21

Now we are ready to get back in the saddle and ride for Jesus!

The End

Notes

Notes

www.ingramcontent.com/pod-product-compliance
Lightning Source LLC
LaVergne TN
LVHW051054080426
835508LV00019B/1877